CONSCIOUS
— CRAFTS —

QUILTING

This book is dedicated to all the quilt makers who so
generously shared their knowledge and love of quiltmaking with me.

First published in 2021 by Leaping Hare Press,
an imprint of The Quarto Group.
The Old Brewery, 6 Blundell Street
London, N7 9BH,
United Kingdom
T (0)20 7700 6700
www.QuartoKnows.com

A catalogue record for this book is available from the British Library.

ISBN 978 0 7112 5745 0
Ebook ISBN 978 0 7112 5746 7

10 9 8 7 6 5 4 3 2

Commissioned by Monica Perdoni
Cover design by Hanri van Wyk
Interior design by Clare Barber
Illustrations by Rob Brandt
Photography by XDB Photography

Printed in China

CONSCIOUS CRAFTS

QUILTING

20 MINDFUL MAKES TO RECONNECT HEAD, HEART & HANDS

Elli Beaven

Leaping Hare Press

contents

introduction

My journey

Mindfulness was not something I was aware of when I started my quilt making journey. I had been given a beautiful quilt for the birth of my daughter and decided I wanted to make one for a friend's first baby. I chose fabric, looked up 'how to make a quilt' and dived in. And that was it, I was hooked. I loved all aspects of the process, from choosing fabric combinations to cutting, piecing and quilting. Although I had learnt to sew as a child, I hadn't sewn for years and loved the challenge of figuring it all out. Quilt making was the perfect antidote both to the long hours on the computer writing a PhD and those spent caring for my daughter. Here was something I could focus on, that engaged my creativity and gave me a sense of accomplishment when everything else felt huge and overwhelming. I didn't know it, but quilt making was exactly what my stressed and anxious soul needed to begin to find some peace.

Quilt making soon became my sanctuary and I turned to it whenever I had the chance, trying out new techniques and patterns, taking classes and building up my skills. Initially I was attracted by the bright, bold prints of commercial quilting cottons but increasingly found myself drawn to the subtler qualities of a textile: it's weave, feel and above all texture. I also began to question the sustainability of commercially produced cotton. Patchwork and quilting were born from the need to utilise every scrap of precious textiles, whether old garments and housewares or the offcuts produced in the garment making process. In these days of a global climate emergency the textile is industry one of the most polluting in the world. Textile waste in the UK comes in at over 200,000 tonnes per year. I realised there was simply no case for not using the abundance of already existing textiles, rather than encouraging the production of new ones. In so doing, I also fell in love with the multilayered richness and depth that repurposed textiles bring to a quilt, their histories of wear and use overlaying my own narratives of finding, cutting and sewing them. Incorporating repurposed textiles into my work was integral to the journey towards finding my own creative voice as a quilt maker.

Mindful quilt making

When I was at school, my handwork teacher taught me to measure my sewing thread by stretching out my left hand holding the end of the thread and cutting it at the point where it reached my heart. There was a practical reason for this - once looped through the eye of the needle the thread will measure roughly the length of the forearm, enabling efficient stitching with minimal arm movements – but more than that it perfectly visualizes the connection of heart and hand that takes place when we fully invest ourselves in creative making. I may not have had much understanding of the concept of mindfulness when I started making quilts, but I absolutely experienced the deeply healing power of connecting heart and hand in the service of creative labour. I kept coming back to quilt making because of how it made me feel, allowing me to release the stresses and noise of the day whilst working creatively to produce a finished item that was both useful and beautiful.

Today I can really appreciate how each part of the quilt making process offers something different. Freeform patchwork is an opportunity to really engage in creative play, experimenting with shape, colour and texture and embracing the raw and imperfect. When I feel energized this is one of my favourite ways to spend time. The methodical process of cutting and piecing squares, on the other hand, is balm to an anxious mind and body when really creative work feels beyond reach. Focusing on this simple repetitive task can really help calm jittery, adrenaline fueled anxiety. Hand quilting is for me the quickest route to finding comfort and quiet. There is something about the feel of the fabrics between my fingers, the weight of the quilt draped over my lap as I stitch that instils a deep sense of calm, no matter the stresses of the day.

This book

Too often we think 'I'm not creative', 'I can't sew' or 'my work isn't good enough' but I hope this book inspires you to dismiss these preconceived ideas. Of course, building skills takes time and practice but anyone can pick up a needle and thread and sew something beautiful and meaningful. Allow yourself some creative playtime, let yourself make mistakes without focusing on the final outcome. Sew for pleasure, finding joy in the pairing of two colours or shapes and the different textures of the fabrics. Take note of what works and what doesn't, what you like and what you don't. Before you know it, you will be making things that you love, that reflect who you are; things that you want to use yourself or give to others.

I actively encourage you to play fast and loose with the patterns in this book. They are made for adapting, for switching binding methods, changing stitching designs, colour placements and sizes. In fact, my primary goal for this book is that in sharing my love of quilt making it encourages and supports your own creative journey; that amongst the projects offered here you find something that kindles your own creative ideas and inspires you to get making.

tools and equipment

Quilting Thread There are many different types of thread available for hand quilting and ultimately which ones you use comes down to personal preference. I would encourage you to try a few different types and see which you prefer.

Thread weights run in reverse order, so the thicker the thread the lower the number. 12, 8 or even 5 weight cotton threads are popular among modern hand quilters, as is Japanese sashiko thread (approximately 5 weight). Standard six-stranded embroidery thread (floss) is usually too thick to get through all the layers of a quilt, but splitting a length into three strands will work fine, if that is what you have available.

Traditional hand quilting thread is a much finer waxed cotton, usually 40 weight. It works well for creating smaller, more precise stitches and for more intricate quilting designs, but does not give the stitch definition and texture that thicker threads do. There are also many different types of silk and linen threads. See what you can find and give it a try – you'll soon work out what you like best.

Sewing Thread This is generally a 40–80 weight thread used for less visible sewing such as piecing or sewing the binding down on the back of a quilt. For piecing, 50 weight cotton is fine, but for bags and pouches I recommend a sturdier standard polyester sew-all thread.

Cutting A rotary cutter, self-healing cutting mat and a couple of quilting rulers will make parts of the quilt-making process quicker and easier but they are by no means essential. The majority of quilting rulers are in inches as this is what the industry works in, though rulers in centimetres can be found. My most used rulers are the 6½in (16.5cm) and 12½in (30.5cm) squares for trimming blocks and a

longer 6 x 24in (15 x 61cm) for cutting strips and squaring up quilts. However, there really is nothing to stop you from getting started with just a pair of scissors, an erasable fabric marker and a simple wooden metre ruler. If a pattern calls for the cutting of multiple shapes of a particular size or the blocks need squaring to a specific size, then simply cut a square of card to the correct size, mark around it with an erasable fabric marker and cut along the lines. The same goes for squaring up a whole quilt – just use a large square of card and the metre ruler, mark your lines and cut with scissors.

Markers An erasable fabric marker is invaluable to the quilt-making process and essential to using the Baptist Fan template (see page 26). Blue water-erasable fabric marker pens are widely available, but for dark fabrics a chalk or ceramic pencil works well too.

For marking straight lines, the Hera marker is a fantastic tool that leaves a just visible, slightly shiny line across the fabric that simply rubs away over time. If you can't find one, a non-serrated, round-ended butter or spreading knife or the pointed end of a knitting needle does the job well.

Seam Allowance This is the distance between the raw edges of the fabrics and the stitching line when sewing two fabrics together. In quilting, the standard is ¼in (6mm), which should be the minimum used. When freeform piecing, especially with fabrics that fray easily, such as linen or more open-weave cottons, you can certainly afford to be a little more generous with your seam allowance. When piecing squares or blocks, such as in the Ad Astra quilt (see page 116), the most important thing is to be consistent with your seam allowance so that all your squares remain roughly the same size. This will make them far easier to sew together.

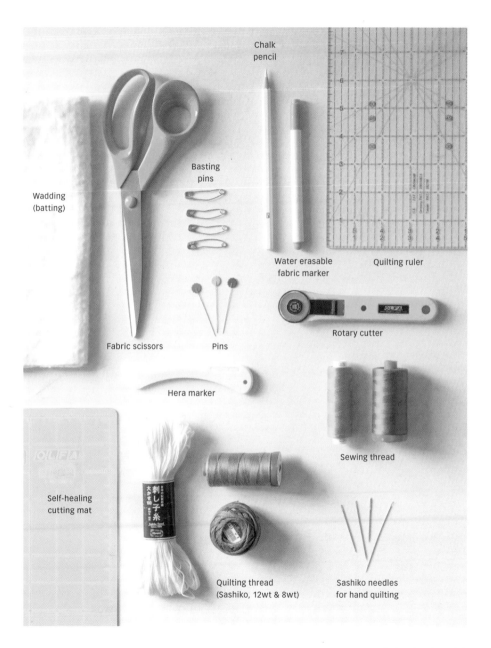

Chalk pencil

Basting pins

Wadding (batting)

Water erasable fabric marker

Quilting ruler

Fabric scissors

Pins

Rotary cutter

Hera marker

Sewing thread

Self-healing cutting mat

Quilting thread (Sashiko, 12wt & 8wt)

Sashiko needles for hand quilting

Pressing Pressing is an integral part of the quilt-making process. Unlike ironing, where you move the iron across the fabric, pressing involves placing the iron onto an area, holding for a few seconds, then lifting and placing on the next part. This prevents the seam allowances shifting, ensuring a nice flat block or quilt top. It is also worth ironing your fabrics before use, as working with wrinkled fabrics is frustrating and they are difficult to cut accurately. Rather than using the steam function of your iron, have a spray bottle of water on hand and spritz areas as you need to.

Pressing Seams Open For the most part in this book, I tell you to press seams open. What this means is pushing the seam allowances to either side of the stitch line. This creates a nice flat patchwork, especially important when working with thicker fabrics such as linen, denim or jersey.

Do this by first running your finger down the seam line to get the fabrics moving in the right direction. This is finger pressing (you can also use a seam roller or the flat end of a Hera marker if you prefer). Then take your seam to the ironing board and press it flat with a hot iron.

Wadding (batting) There are many different types of wadding (batting) available and it's worth trying a few or getting some samples to see which you prefer. I would always recommend a natural fibre wadding (batting), although from a sustainable angle the recycled cotton/polyester (70/30) blend is probably the best option.

Cotton wadding (batting) comes in different thicknesses (called loft), but bear in mind that a thicker, denser wadding (batting) will be that much harder to hand quilt. Bamboo or bamboo-blend wadding (batting) is lighter with a good drape, while wool wadding (batting) tends to be light with quite a high loft, making it a popular choice with hand quilters. Check that the wool is super wash, though, or be prepared to only cold hand wash any quilts made with untreated wool wadding (batting). Most other wadding (batting) can be machine washed cool once inside a fully quilted and bound quilt.

Quilt Backs In all the materials lists in this book you'll find the dimensions of quilt backing fabric necessary for that project. However, this should not stop you from getting creative with your quilt backs – in fact, this is precisely where you have the freedom to really get creative.

Use up odd leftover blocks, pieces of treasured print (the perfect place for a big bold print that is too pretty to cut up) or the leftovers from a quilt top. Sew together as larger pieces or use up your tiniest scraps – if there are no real rules to quilt-making, there are absolutely no rules to making quilt backs. I love a neat and tidy quilt top that hides a riotous backside and I can't tell you how many times I've ended up loving the back even more than the front!

Quilt Care and Labelling Depending on the wadding (batting), most quilts can be hand or gently machine washed and dried flat or on the line once bound and finished. If you used spray baste or drew out your quilting lines with a water erasable marker, washing will remove both. The first wash will often shrink the wadding (batting) slightly, giving that crinkled texture found in antique quilts. Many hours of care and attention go into a quilt and it is important to honour the time and love you have invested in the making process. I add my initials and the year in free-hand stitches as well as a printed logo from my studio but you could use a permanent marker, printed labels or embroider a label directly onto the quilt back.

useful techniques
running stitch

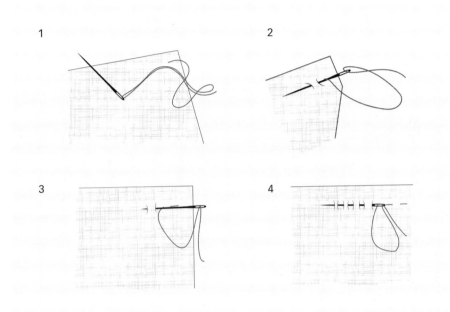

Running stitch is the simplest of stitches and the basis of all hand sewing.

1 Knot your thread and bring the needle through from the back of the fabric to the front so the knot stays in the back.

2 Take the needle forward one stitch length, push the tip through to the back, scoop up one stitch length of fabric and push the needle back through to the front. Grasp the pointed end of the needle and pull the needle all the way through until the thread is taut.

3 Move forward one stitch length and repeat this process.

4 Once you gain confidence, you can load multiple stitches onto your needle in one go, moving from front to back, to front to back.

5 When you have finished stitching, bring your needle through to the back, take a small stitch on the spot, pulling it through only enough to leave a small loop. Pass the needle though the loop and pull the thread tight. Repeat and cut the thread, leaving a ½in (1.3cm) tail.

ladder stitch

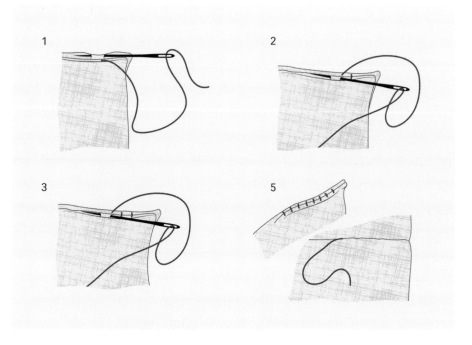

Ladder stitch, also known as slip stitch, is used for the almost invisible attaching of two fabrics. I use it to sew down the quilt binding on the back of a quilt, but it also works to close a broken seam or turning gap in the lining of a bag. Use a coordinating sewing thread.

1 Knot the end of the thread and bury in the seam allowance, bringing the needle up where you wish to start. Take a small stitch along the fold of one side.

2 Cross to the other side and start the next stitch at the point where the stitch ended on the other side.

3 Take a small stitch and cross back to the first side.

4 Continue stitching like this, creating small straight stitches across the seam that look like the rungs of a ladder. As you pull the thread tight, the stitches will disappear, leaving you with a virtually invisible seam.

basting

Tools and materials
- Quilt top
- Backing fabric
- Top fabric
- Wadding (batting)
- Masking tape
- Basting pins, basting spray or sewing thread

Basting is the layering and securing of the three components that make up a quilt: the backing fabric, wadding (batting) and quilt top. There are several different ways of basting, but they all start with same process of layering and smoothing, and have the ultimate goal of a secure and wrinkle-free quilt sandwich, ready for quilting.

making the quilt sandwich

When your quilt sandwich is complete, you can choose one of the following options below for securing the three layers together: thread basting, pin basting or spray basting. If you opt for thread or pin basting, you will find it easier to mark out any quilting designs onto the quilt top at the quilt sandwich stage.

1 Begin by laying out the freshly pressed quilt back, right side down, on the floor or a large table. Tape it down in a couple of places on each side, gently straightening the fabric as you go. Take care not to stretch or distort the fabric.

2 Centre the wadding (batting) over the quilt back, smoothing out any wrinkles. It should sit well inside the backing fabric. (Stop here if you plan on spray basting your quilt.)

3 Lay the pressed quilt top, right side up, over the wadding (batting) and smooth out any wrinkles. There should be 1–2in (2.5–5cm) of wadding (batting) visible around the whole quilt top.

1

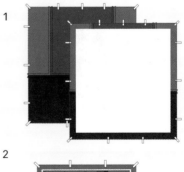

2

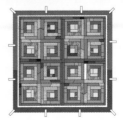

thread basting

This is the oldest and most low-tech way of securing the three layers of a quilt, requiring nothing but a needle and thread. Contrasting thread will help when it comes to removing the stitches once you have finished quilting. A long needle will make taking large stitches that much easier. Remember to mark out your quilting lines before thread basting.

1 With the quilt sandwich still taped in place, begin in the centre of the quilt with a roughly ½in (1.3cm) stitch. There's no need to knot the end of your thread, just leave 1–2in (2.5–5cm) of tail as you pull it through and take a second stitch over the first one to secure.

2 Take another ½in (1.3cm) stitch, about 3–4in (7.5–10cm) directly below the first stitch.

3 Continue stitching like this until you reach the outer edge of the quilt.

4 Take a 3–4in (7.5–10cm) stitch to the left side and begin another row of basting stitches, this time working upwards, parallel to the first line.

5 When you reach the point where you started the first line, take another large stitch to the left and work your way back down again.

6 When the thread runs out, simply leave a tail and start the new thread at the next stitch, as you did in Step 1.

7 Continue until you reach the outer edge of the quilt. Make sure the last row of basting stitches sits right at the edge of the quilt top.

8 Baste the remaining three quadrants in the same way.

1

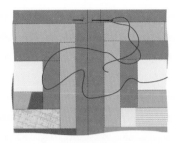

2

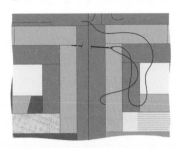

3

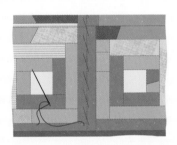

4

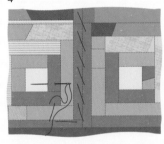

5

7

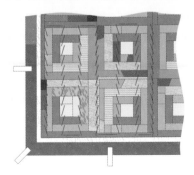

spray basting

Spray baste is a temporary spray adhesive that is sprayed onto the wadding (batting), effectively sticking the layers of the quilt sandwich together. I'm not generally a fan of products with so much single-use packaging, but I also cannot deny that spray basting has come to the rescue with some particularly tricky quilts. It makes for a very stable quilt sandwich, which is especially useful when basting a quilt made from more shifty fabrics such as linen, viscose, rayon, fine silks or stretch fabrics. It's also very useful for quickly basting small projects. Follow the instructions for Making the Quilt Sandwich up to Step 2 (see page 13), then continue with the following steps.

1 Keeping the wadding (batting) in position on the quilt back, fold it in half and spray the exposed half with basting spray, as described on the instructions on the can.

2 Fold the wadding (batting) back over the quilt back, smoothing it down with your hands.

3 Repeat for the other side, folding the wadding (batting) back, spraying it and smoothing it back down.

4 Now add the quilt top, right side up. Centre it onto the wadding (batting) and ensure it is completely smooth, with 1–2in (2.5–5cm) of wadding (batting) visible around the whole top.

5 Fold half the quilt top back over itself and spray the exposed wadding (batting) with basting spray. For larger quilts, spray a 15–20in (38–51cm) strip across the width.

6 Lay the quilt top back over the sprayed wadding (batting), smoothing as you go. If any wrinkles form, just lift the quilt top away from the wadding (batting) and replace. For larger quilts, repeat Steps 5 and 6 until you reach the edge.

7 Fold the other side over and repeat the process, spraying, folding back and smoothing as you go.

8 The quilt is now ready for marking quilt lines and quilting. Once the quilt is completely finished, wash to remove the spray baste.

1

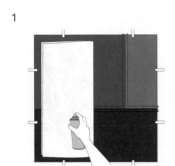

2

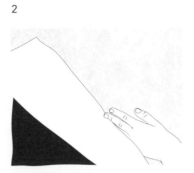

4

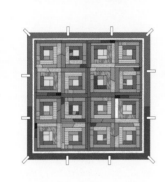

5

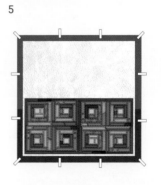

6

binding

pin basting

Pin basting is a little quicker than thread basting. You can buy specially curved basting safety pins that help you scoop up the three layers as you pin but ordinary large safety pins work fine too. Be sure to mark your quilting lines out before you pin baste.

1   Starting in the centre of the taped down quilt sandwich, push the pins through all three layers, at 3–5in (7.5–12.5cm) intervals across the quilt. Try not to pin across any marked quilting lines.

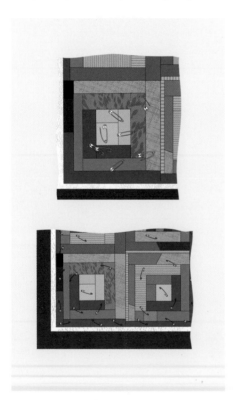

double fold binding

Traditional double fold binding adds another fabric to your quilt by creating a frame for the front and back. The front is sewn down with a sewing machine and then hand finished with a ladder stitch on the reverse. The most common width is 2½in (6.5cm), but it's worth trying out different sizes.

1   Measure the four sides of your finished quilt and add approximately 12in (30cm) to this length – this will be the amount of binding you will need for your quilt. Bear in mind that each time you join two strips, you will lose 2½in (6.5cm) in length.

2   Cut your binding fabric into the necessary quantity of 2½in (6.5cm) strips.

3   Join the first two strips by laying the ends right sides together at 90 degrees. Mark a line diagonally, corner to corner, and pin to secure.

4   Sew along the line and then trim away the excess, leaving a ¼in (6mm) seam allowance. Repeat until you have joined all the strips.

5   Press the joining seams open and then press the length of binding in half, wrong sides together.

6   Starting in the centre of one side, align the raw edge of the binding with the raw edge of the quilt. Leaving a 6–8in (15–20cm) tail, begin sewing the binding down using a ¼in (6mm) seam. Backstitch at the beginning. If you sew slowly, stopping regularly to ensure the raw edges of the binding and quilt are aligned, there is no need to use pins.

7   When you reach the first corner, stop sewing ¼in (6mm) from the bottom edge. Leave the needle down, rotate the quilt 45 degrees and sew the remaining stitches into the corner and off the edge of the quilt.

2

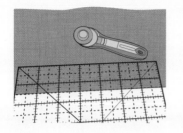

3

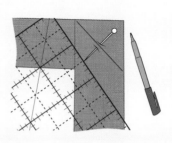

4

5

6

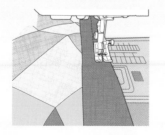

7

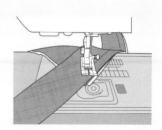

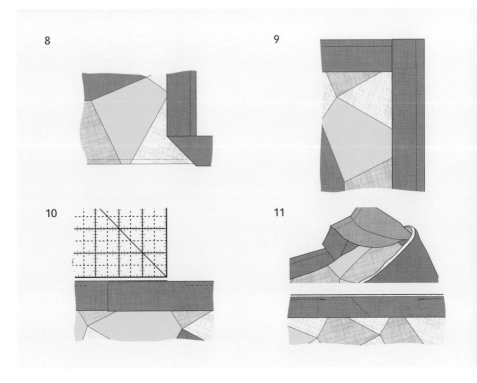

8   Lift the presser foot and pull the quilt slightly forward. Fold the binding to the right at 45 degrees along the sewn line, then fold it back down so that the raw edge aligns with the next side of the quilt and the fold with the previously sewn edge so that the fold aligns neatly with the raw edge that you have just sewn.

9   Rotate the quilt slightly and sew the binding down on the next edge, starting right at the fold. Starting from the very edge of the quilt, begin sewing down the next side. Continue around the edge of the quilt, following Steps 7–9 for each corner, and stopping approximately 12in (30cm) from where you started. Backstitch and remove from the machine.

10 Lay the quilt out flat and overlap the two ends of the binding. In the centre of the unsewn gap, measure 2½in (6cm) (or the chosen width of your binding) of overlap and trim away the remainder.

11 Lay the two ends at right angles, right sides together, then mark a line, pin and join as you did in Steps 3 and 4. Finger press the seam open and refold the binding in half. The binding should now cover the unsewn gap perfectly. Sew it down, backstitching at the beginning and end.

12

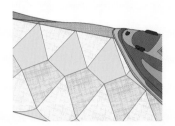

14

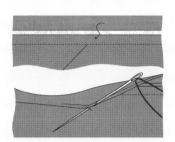

15a

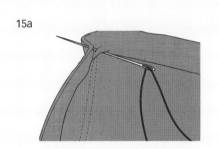

15b

12 Press the binding up towards the raw edge all the way around the quilt.

13 Fold the binding over to the back, encasing the raw edges of the quilt and covering the seam created when it was sewn to the front of the quilt. You can use clips or pins to secure it in place before you hand sew it down, but I prefer to fold it over as I go, holding a few inches in place with my left hand.

14 Use a fine sewing thread that blends with the binding fabric. Bury the knot above the binding seam line and bring the needle up just below it. Use a ladder stitch to sew the binding down, running the needle through the fold of the

binding then into the quilt back. Take care that your stitches only go through the backing fabric and wadding (batting), not all the way through to the front.

15 When you reach a corner, stop stitching ¼in (6mm) away from the edge and fold the next side over to create a neat mitred corner. Take a couple of extra stitches into the corner to secure it, and continue to the next side.

16 When you reach the end, take several small stitches as close under the binding as you can and finish by burying your thread tail a few inches away. Trim and your quilt is done!

binding from the reverse

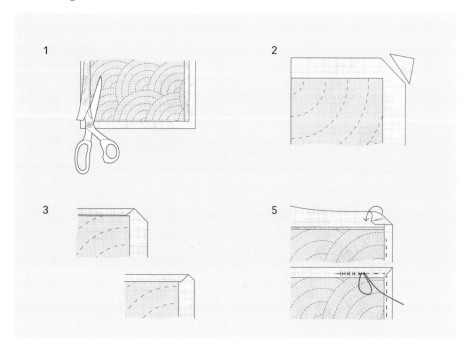

This method brings any additional backing fabric to the front of the quilt to create the binding.

1 Trim your quilted piece so that the top fabric and wadding (batting) are the same size, with the backing fabric an even 1in (2.5cm) (or ¾in (2cm) on small projects) larger on all sides.

2 Mark 1in (2.5cm) (or ¾in (2cm) on small projects) in from each corner. Connect the marks with a diagonal line and cut along it to remove the corners.

3 Create a binding by folding the binding fabric in half towards the quilted part. Crease the fabric with your finger or use a hot iron to press flat. Fold it over again to encase the raw edge.

4 Sew it down using a visible running stitch or an invisible ladder stitch. Start in the centre of one side and bury your knot under the binding. For a visible running stitch, use quilting thread to sew close to the edge of the binding, ensuring your stitches go through to the back. For an invisible ladder stitch, use a fine coordinating thread and only stitch through the top fabric and wadding.

5 Stop ½in (1.3cm) from the corner. Rotate the piece clockwise and fold the corner of the binding inwards. Fold the binding fabric down twice, to create a neat mitred corner. Continue stitching, securing the corner with an extra stitch as you go. Repeat with the other corners until you reach your starting point. Use the last stitch on the reverse to bury your knot and tail.

hand piecing vs. machine piecing

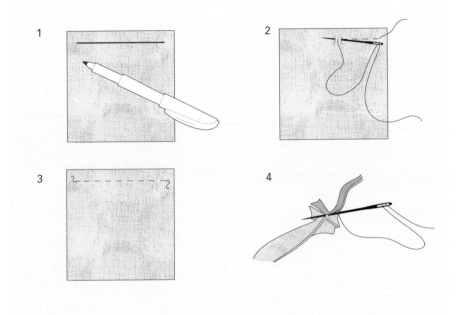

For most of the projects in this book I use a sewing machine to sew the fabrics together as this is the quickest way of doing it. That said, there is nothing to stop you choosing to sew those seams by hand and any seam that is sewn on a sewing machine can be hand pieced. This is done using a simple running stitch and short stitch length.

1 Lay your fabrics right sides together with the raw edges aligned. You will use a ¼in (6mm) seam allowance and you can mark your stitching line with a pencil on the back of one side.

2 Start stitching ¼in (6mm) in. You can knot your thread or simply take two small stitches on the same spot (backstitch) to start. Sew the seam with a running stitch. Some sewers like to take a backstitch every few inches for extra security.

3 Stop ¼in (6mm) from the end of the seam, finishing your thread with either a knot or another backstitch.

4 When joining pieces with a seam, do not stitch through the seam allowance, instead bring the needle through at a slight angle to avoid catching the seam allowance.

hand quilting

Hand quilting is essentially a running stitch that goes through all three layers of the quilt, securing them together. As long as your stitches perform this function, everything else in terms of style, tools and techniques is personal preference. Hand quilting a quilt takes many, many hours so finding a method that is comfortable for you is especially important. If the technique I use, described below, does not work for you, don't hesitate to explore the many other approaches to hand quilting offered by other quilt makers.

1 Knot your thread and bring the needle through from the back at an angle to the point where you want to start quilting. Pull the thread through and keep pulling until you feel the knot 'pop' through the backing fabric to rest in the wadding (batting).

2 Place your left hand underneath the area you want to quilt. Take the first stitch by pointing the needle almost vertically down and pushing it through to the back.

3 Once the tip of the needle comes out at the back, bring the needle back to the horizontal again. Using the middle finger of your left hand, push the needle flat against the backing fabric, while the left-hand thumb and forefinger pinch the quilt sandwich and pull it downwards against the middle finger, creating tension.

4 At the same time, push the needle forward along the quilting line and it will come back out on the front, one stitch length away.

5 Repeat for the next stitch, pointing the needle almost vertically down, pushing it through to the back, pulling the quilt downwards in front of the needle and then pushing the needle through to come back to the front.

6 As you grow in confidence, you can load multiple stitches onto your needle before pulling the thread through.

7 Continue quilting until your thread is around 2–3in (5–7.5cm), finishing on the back side. Remove the needle, and rethread with a new thread. Do not knot your new thread, but lay the end together with the thread tail of the last and tie a loose knot. Do not pull tight yet.

8 Put the point of the needle through the knot loop and place it one stitch length away from where the thread tail comes up. Now gently tighten the knot loop, pushing it down to the point of the needle.

9 Take the needle away and tighten the knot fully – it should be sitting one stitch length away from the base of the tail.

10 Take the next stitch back through to the front, pulling the thread all the way through. Continue pulling until you feel the knot 'pop' through the fabric into the wadding (batting).

11 You can either continue quilting and bury all the tails at the end, or do them as you go along. Take a large-eyed needle, thread with both tails and take the needle through the hole that the tails come from, into the wadding (batting) for 1–2in (2.5–4cm) and back up to the back of the quilt. Trim any leftover thread tail close to the quilt surface and rub gently to make it disappear below the fabric.

12 If the thread tails are too short to thread onto a needle, take the needle through the hole, into the wadding (batting) and back up again, leaving the eye poking out of the hole. Thread the tails through the eye and finish pulling the needle through. Trim as before.

2

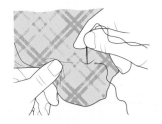

3–4

5–6

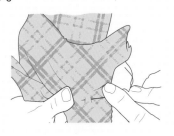

7

9

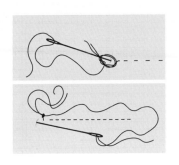

11

baptist fan template

Tools and materials
- 1in (2.5cm) wide by 6–8in (15–20cm) long strip of template plastic or sturdy card
- Pin
- Small, sharp-pointed scissors
- Erasable fabric marker
- Ruler (if using card)

The Baptist Fan – a traditional quilting design – is one of my favourites, and I often use the design-marking template in the projects in this book. It's a simple template to make and can be used in many different ways.

making a template

1 Cut your card or template plastic into a 1in (2.5cm) wide strip. The longer the strip, the more arcs you can draw in each set but aim for a minimum of 6.5in (15cm) in length.

2 If you're using card, draw a line marking the centre down the length of the strip then measure ¼in (6mm) in from one short end and draw a line. Where the line intersects with the centre line is the pin point. Now mark lines at 1in (2.5cm) intervals from the pin point along the length of the card strip. These lines are already marked on the template plastic.

3 Use a pin to push through each of the marked points at 1in (2.5cm) intervals.

4 Leaving the first pin-hole (pin point) as it is, use the sharp point of a small pair of scissors to slightly enlarge each of the remaining pin-holes. Take care not to enlarge them too much – they only need to fit the tip of the erasable fabric marker. Be sure to enlarge the holes from the same side, so that all the rough edges end up on the front, leaving a smooth back side that won't snag your fabric as you use the template.

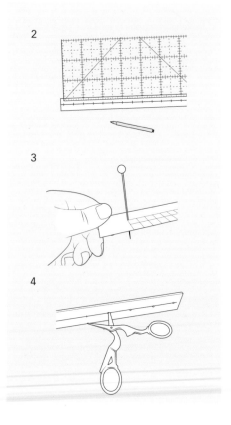

2

3

4

using the baptist fan template

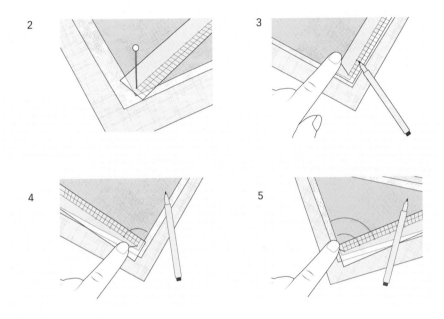

2

3

4

5

This is how to draw out a traditional Baptist Fan design. It is helpful to draw out a square or rectangle about ¼in (6mm) in from the raw edges of the top fabric so that you have a clear area within which to draw out your design. This also ensures that when trimming the quilt, ready for binding, you will not have to cut through any quilting stitches.

1 Layer your front fabric, wadding (batting) and backing fabric as if ready for basting (see Making the Quilt Sandwich, page 13), but do not baste.

2 Put a pin through the pin point of the template from front to back and place the point in the bottom right-hand corner of your prepared fabric.

3 Hold the end of the pin in place with one hand and, with the other, place the erasable fabric marker tip through the first scissor hole and on to the fabric.

4 Start at the vertical edge of the quilt and draw your first arc down to the horizontal edge.

5 Move the marker to the next hole along and draw the next arc from the horizontal edge to the vertical edge. Move the marker up another hole and draw the next arc by sliding the template back to the horizontal edge. Continue until you have the desired number of arcs.

6　Start the next set of arcs where the outer arc of the preceding set intersects with the bottom edge. Put the pin through the template and into the fabric and wadding (batting) layer. Hold in place with one hand and use the other to draw out the next set of arcs. Continue in this way until you reach the edge of the fabric – you may have to finish with some partial arcs.

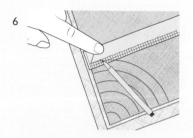

7　Begin the next row of arcs above the first one on the right-hand edge, using the intersection of the outer arc with the vertical edge as the pin point and stopping each arc when it meets the top of the row below.

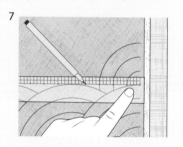

stitching the baptist fan design

Stitching the design in this way will enable you to stitch continuously, minimizing cutting and restarting. The aim is to finish the quilting of each arc in a place where you can easily continue to the next arc.

1　Begin quilting in the bottom right-hand corner, where you started drawing the design. If you have an even number of arcs in each set, begin from the bottom end of the first arc. If you have an odd number of arcs in each set you will need to begin from the top end of the first arc.

2　Bring the needle up at 1 and quilt along the first small arc.

3　When you reach the end, slide the needle between the front and back layers of the quilt and bring the needle up at 2.

4　Quilt the next arc, again sliding the needle between the quilt layers when you reach the end. Bring the needle up at 3 and continue quilting the first row of arcs in this way across the width of the quilt.

5　When you reach the end of the row, knot and cut your thread and start the next row up from the right-hand side, beginning with smallest arc, as you did before.

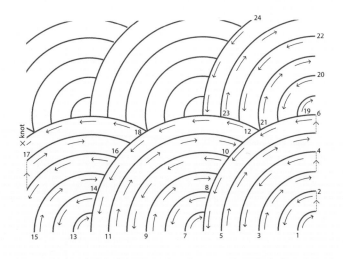

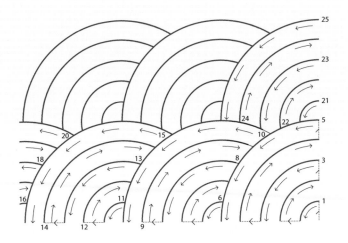

Above: Odd (lower) and even (upper) number of arcs per set.

freeform patchwork

Freeform patchwork involves the intuitive piecing of fabrics without following a pattern or design. It is a wonderfully creative and playful process that embraces imperfections and is especially well-suited to the kind of odd-shaped pieces of fabric and the variety of textures and fabric weights generated by repurposing textiles. Although there are no real rules, there are several factors worth keeping in mind as you sew:

Colour Your choice of palette can really impact the look of the finished piece. Patchwork can quickly become busy and bringing many colours and prints into a piece will exacerbate this so choose your colour palette thoughtfully. If you are well versed in the use of colour then this will come easily to you, but don't worry if you are not. Keep practising, playing with different combinations of colours to see how they work together.

Scale Experiment with different sized pieces of fabric to explore how they affect the overall look of your piece or try cutting up different scale prints. Balancing areas of smaller piecing or print with larger single pieces of plain fabric can give the eye somewhere to rest.

Shape Grouping shapes together or using a limited number of shapes can help bring an element of order. Mixing them all up can result in a more dynamic effect but can easily become messy and chaotic without care. Trimming all your patchwork pieces to the same size before joining them together is another way of introducing an element of order or calm to more random piecing.

strips freeform patchwork

1 Sew together two strips of any width. If one strip is longer, trim away the excess.

2 Finger press the seam open and add another strip. Repeat like this until you reach the desired length.

3 If, when you are arranging the sections, you decide the strip is perhaps too wide, simply cut in half and join the two ends to make a longer, narrower section. You can repeat this process to create a thin strip of what are now small squares. This can be used as a border or sandwiched between two plain fabrics to make a striped strip.

4 You can also take a section of pieced strips and cut it into triangles, squares on point or any number of different shapes.

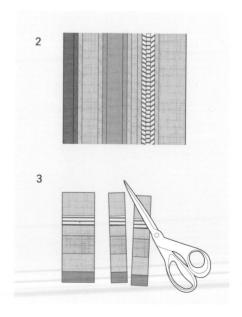

half square triangles freeform patchwork

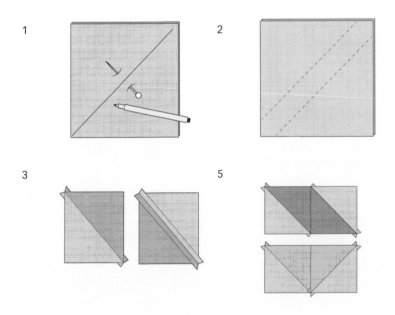

1 Place two squares right sides together and mark a line diagonally across from corner to corner.

2 Sew a seam ¼in (6mm) in, either side of the marked line.

3 Cut along the marked line and press the seams open. If you want more precise squares, trim with a ruler, or use as they are.

4 Include the edge being trimmed away on one side.

5 Depending how you join them you can make a triangle strip or border, diamond shapes or 'flying geese', a traditional quilt block.

basic freeform patchwork

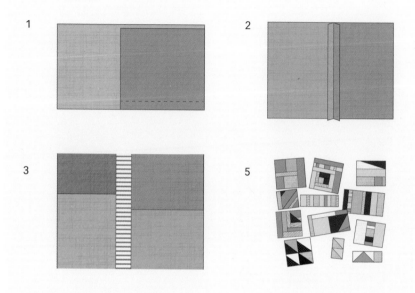

1

2

3

5

1 Begin by choosing your colour palette and place your pile of fabric pieces next to the sewing machine. Take two pieces and sew, right sides together, with a ¼in (6mm) seam allowance.

2 If one piece is a lot larger than the other, trim away the excess. Finger press the seam open, pushing the seam allowances to either side.

3 Take another piece and add it to either of the first pieces. Finger press the seam open. If you want to add a smaller piece, cut one from a larger piece with scissors and add it as before. If a piece is not long enough, join it to another before adding it. Continue like this until you are happy with the arrangement. It does not matter what size it is for now. Press with an iron and put to one side.

4 Start a new composition, joining smaller pieces in the same way to build up a larger piece.

5 Once you have a few compositions, and depending on the final size you are aiming for, lay them out and see how they work together. If it's a bit busy, add in some larger single pieces of fabric to give the eye somewhere to rest.

6 Once you're happy, find an arrangement that works and begin joining sections. At this stage it is helpful to straighten the edges using a ruler and rotary cutter or scissors to keep everything lying flat once sewn together. You may also need to add small pieces to make everything fit together. After each section joining seam, press it open with an iron. Keep going until you reach your desired size.

repurposing fabric

Repurposing clothing or household textiles for making quilts is an idea as old as quilt making itself. It remains the most sustainable and cost-effective way to make a quilt but there is much more to repurposing than environmental and economic concerns. When you bring used and worn textiles into your work you connect it with a wider narrative, from the memories imbued in each piece of cloth to the physical traces of their use in patches of wear and fading. Irrespective of whether it is imagined or your own, each garment or piece of used textile has a story, and their use will bring richness and depth to your quilts. From a purely aesthetic point of view, you will achieve far greater variety and originality in pattern, colour and texture than you would ever be able to with commercially produced quilting cottons. Sourcing textiles for reuse can also be a wonderful process in itself and before long you will be eyeing up every garment for its quilt potential. It's easy to quickly build up a large stash of fabrics, so the sooner you understand which textiles work for you the more discerning you can be. As you go round a charity shop or car boot sale, touch the fabrics and clothing that you see, learn to distinguish between the different fibres so that as you build a small collection of textiles to work with you also school yourself in exactly what you like and what you can manage to work with.

The main things to remember when sourcing and using repurposed textiles:

1 Stick with natural fibres – cotton, linen, wool and silk. These can all be pressed with a hot iron making them better suited to the quilt making process. They also feel nicer and are biodegradable.

2 Wash everything well before use. If it can't withstand a standard wash in the washing machine you don't want to put it in a quilt made for everyday use.

3 If you're new to sewing and making quilts, cotton and cotton/linen blend fabrics are the easiest to work with – the men's shirt section is a great place to start.

4 Always use a lightweight fusible interfacing on very fine or stretch fabrics before using.

5 Cut garments apart by cutting either side of seams, either lying flat on a mat with a rotary cutter or by hand with scissors. Put collars, plackets, cuffs and seams in the textile waste bin* but pockets and other detailing can add interest to your quilt. Darts, such as those in the back of a fitted shirt, can be carefully unpicked or kept as they are to create interest.

* A note on textile waste
Keep a separate bin where you work for all your textile waste – trimmings from blocks and quilts, shirt collars/plackets etc. When full, either put in a textile recycling bin or use as stuffing for soft toys and cushions, chopping up any larger pieces. See the Waste Not Floor Cushion for how to make a cushion insert. The same goes for any accidentally felted wool sweaters or those eaten beyond repair by moths (after washing and freezing, of course).

quilted coasters

These coasters are essentially miniature quilts. They require minimal tools and materials and are relatively quick to sew, making them a great way to begin your exploration of the quilting process. As your confidence grows, they are also a wonderful way to try out ideas – small experiments in shape, colour and texture – whose functional use will continue to bring joy to your home for years to come.

Materials

Measures: 4¼in (10.5cm) square

- Four 4in (10cm) squares top fabric
- Four 4in (10cm) squares wadding (batting)
- Four 5½in (14cm) squares backing/ binding fabric
- Quilting thread

to make

1 Place a 4in (10cm) square of top fabric right side up over a wadding (batting) square. Use a ruler and an erasable fabric marker to draw a 1in (2.5cm) grid on the fabric.

2 Cut about 25in (64cm) of quilting thread and, starting in the lower right-hand corner, begin to stitch plus signs, starting with the horizontal lines. Bring the needle through from the back, just before where the right-hand vertical line crosses the bottom horizontal line. Take a ¼in (6mm) stitch over the vertical line, bringing the needle through to the back just after where the lines intersect. Take two further stitches along the bottom horizontal line, each crossing over the point where the lines intersect. This will require taking a larger stitch on the reverse.

3 For the second row of stitches, take a larger vertical stitch on the reverse to bring the needle through to the front, just before where the left-hand vertical line intersects with the middle horizontal line, and continue as before. Repeat for the third horizontal line.

4 Rotate the square 90 degrees so your horizontal stitches are now vertical. Beginning in the corner where you made the last stitch, continue stitching as you did before, only now with each stitch crossing over the previous ones to create nine plus shapes. When you finish the final stitch, knot and trim your thread on the reverse.

5 Place the quilted square wrong sides together in the centre of a 5½in (14cm) backing fabric square and use a couple of pins in the centre to secure. There should be an even ¾in (2cm) of backing fabric excess on all sides.

6 Now follow the binding from reverse tutorial in the Useful Techniques section (see page 22) to complete the coasters, sewing the binding down using the visible running stitch method.

7 Repeat steps 1–6 for the remaining coasters.

notice the detail

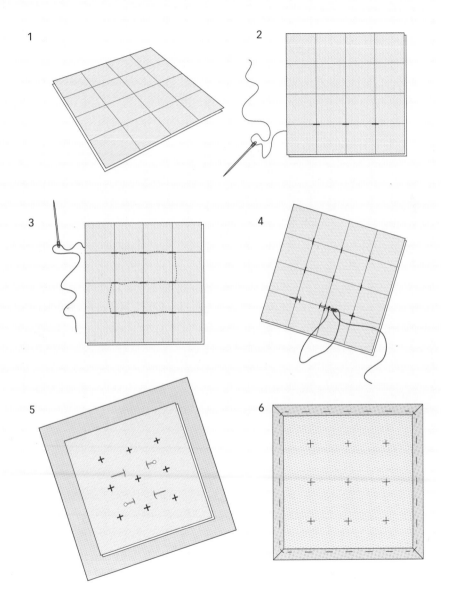

1

2

3

4

5

6

strips trivet

Trivet is such a mundane word, really these are little pieces of art for your table, kitchen, wall or wherever else you choose to put them. It is a good project for dipping your toe into freeform patchwork piecing. The key is not to overthink it. Join pieces, see how the colours work together and if they're not speaking to you just put it aside and start another. A small project like this is perfect for bringing a bit of creativity to your day, allowing the busy thoughts of the day to recede as you absorb yourself in the interplay of colour, shape and texture.

Materials
Measures: 8½in (22cm) square

- Strips of fabric, minimum 1in (2.5cm) wide to make up four 4½in (11cm) squares
- 8½in (22cm) square of insulated wadding (batting) (or use two 8½in (22cm) squares of regular wadding/batting)
- 10½in (27cm) square of backing/binding fabric
- Quilting thread

to make

1
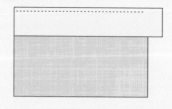

2
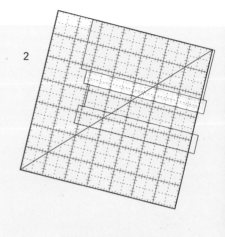

3

4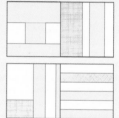

1 Begin by sewing two strips, right sides together, along their long edges. If any strips are shorter than 4½in (11cm), simply join two strips at their short ends to create a longer strip and use in the same way. Finger press the seam open.

2 Keep adding strips until your piece is at least 4½in (11cm) square.

3 Trim to 4½in (11cm) square. Repeat for the remaining three squares and press.

4 Lay out your squares, alternating the direction of the strips. Sew together by piecing into pairs

and then joining the pairs to make one 8½in (22cm) square.

5 Layer the pieced square over the square of wadding (batting) and then centre them over the square of backing fabric. There should be 1in (2.5cm) of backing fabric visible along each edge. Baste in place using your preferred method (see pages 13–18).

6 Measure 1½in (3.8cm) in from the edge of the pieced square and draw a line with an erasable marker. Do the same around the whole edge to

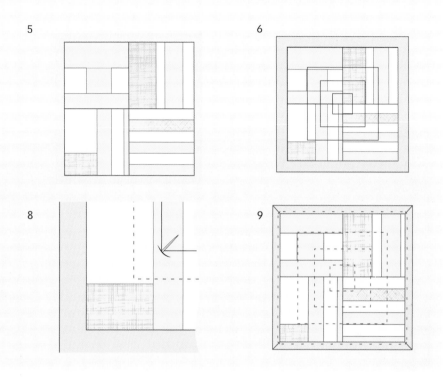

5

6

8

9

create a square. Repeat 1in (2.5cm) in from the drawn lines to create another square, and once more 1in (2.5cm) within that to create a small square in the centre.

7 Quilt these squares, starting with the outer square. Bring the needle up in the lower right-hand corner of the square. Quilt along it, ensuring your stitches go all the way through to the back. You may find with the extra thickness that it is easier to take one stitch at a time, rather than loading the needle with several in one go.

8 When you are back to where you started, bring the needle through to the back and take the final stitch, turning the needle at an angle through the wadding (batting) so that it reaches the front at the corner of the next quilting line. Continue in this way until you have quilted all the lines, using the last stitch on the back to bury your knot

9 Follow the binding from reverse tutorial in the Useful Techniques section (see page 22) to complete the trivet, using the visible running stitch method to sew the binding down.

needle book

Every sewer needs somewhere to store their
needles and this soft and tactile needle book
is a good place to start. It's a relatively simple
make and the perfect opportunity to try out the
Baptist Fan template (see page 26) and practice
your ladder stitch binding finish. Whether you
make this for yourself or as a gift, there is such
a unique joy in the everyday use of something
that has been carefully and thoughtfully made
by hand.

Materials
Measures: 4½in
(11.5cm) square

- 4½ x 9in (11 x 23cm)
  top fabric
- 4½ x 9in (11 x 23cm)
  wadding (batting)
- 6 x 10½in (15 x 27cm)
  backing/binding fabric
- 4 x 7¾in (10 x 20cm)
  felt
- Quilting thread
- Sewing thread
  to match the back/
  binding fabric
- Baptist Fan template
  (see page 26)

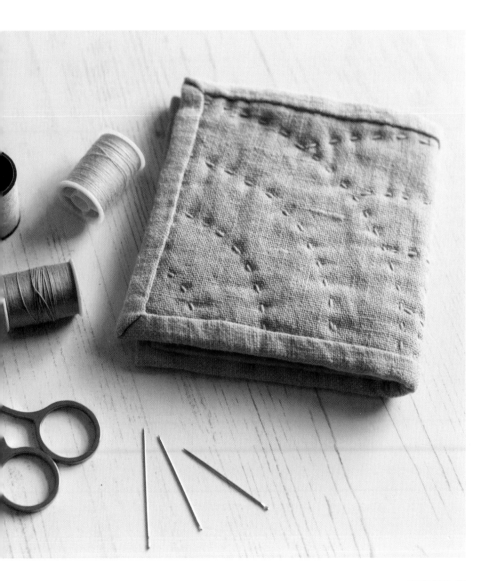

to make

1 Place the top fabric right side up on the wadding (batting), then lay both on the wrong side of the backing fabric, ensuring an even border of ¾in (1.9cm) all around. Use pins or basting spray to secure the layers together (see pages 16–18).

2 Follow the instructions for using the Baptist Fan template (see page 26) to mark out the quilting lines on the top fabric.

3 Quilt the design in your chosen colour, following the Baptist Fan stitch guide. Remember that both sides will be visible so finish each arc neatly, running the thread between the layers to reach the next arc and burying knots in the wadding (batting).

4 Once you have completed the quilting design, use the binding from reverse tutorial (see page 22) to complete the binding. Use coordinating sewing thread and the invisible ladder stitch method to sew the binding down.

5 With an erasable fabric marker, mark the centre of each of the long sides on the reverse of the quilted panel and draw a line down the centre of the piece of felt. Line up the centre line on the felt with the centre marks on the quilted panel and pin in place.

6 Using a thread that matches the colour of the front fabric, sew a running stitch along the centre line to secure the felt in place.

7 Fold in half and your needle book is complete.

embrace the beauty of the handmade

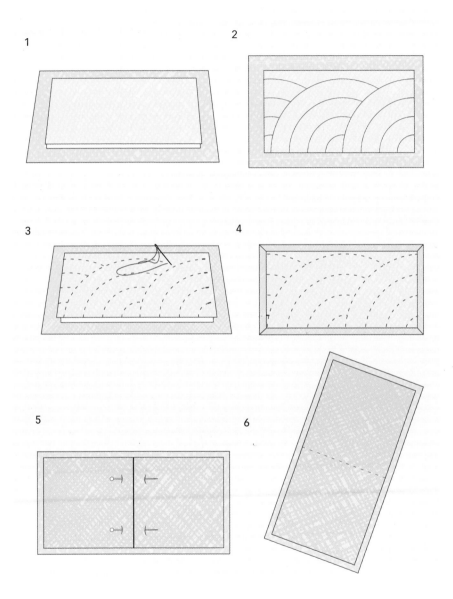

1

2

3

4

5

6

storage basket

Materials
Measures: 6¾ x 11¾ x 5½in (17 x 30 x 14cm)

- 24½ x 11½in (62 x 29cm) outer fabric
- 24½ x 11½in (62 x 29cm) lining fabric (heavier weight)
- 24½ x 11½in (62 x 29cm) wadding (batting)
- Quilting thread

The gentle rhythm of simple straight line quilting is a wonderful way to fill a quiet moment in your day. And when you're done, this quilted storage basket can be used to hold any number of things – knitting projects, fabric scraps, threads, yarn, toys ... the list goes on! They say a tidy house makes for a tidy mind and this project certainly gives you the opportunity for both. Using a heavier-weight linen, canvas or denim for the lining will help the basket hold its shape.

to make

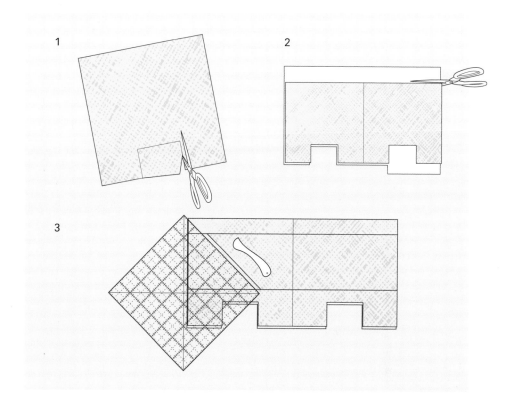

1 With the outer fabric folded in half, measure 3¾in (9.6cm) from the fold along the bottom raw edge and mark a rectangle 4½in (11cm) wide by 2½in (6.5cm) high. Remove, cutting through both layers of fabric. Repeat for the lining fabric.

2 Open out and place the outer fabric, right side up, onto the wadding (batting). Baste, then trim the wadding (batting) to match the fabrics, including removing it from cut-out areas.

3 Mark a line 1½in (3.8cm) from the top raw edge and another 3½in (9cm) from the bottom raw edge. Between these two lines mark a diagonal line at 45 degrees. Use this line to mark out diagonal lines 1in (2.5cm) apart across the length of the fabric.

4 Beginning at one end, quilt the diagonal lines, starting and ending each line of stitches neatly at the top and bottom horizontal lines.

5 Once you have finished quilting, fold the panel in half, right sides together, and join the sides with a ½in (1.3cm) seam. Press open.

4

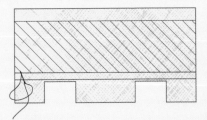

6 Rotate the seam into the centre so the two bottom sections align. Sew them together and press open.

7 Create the base of the basket by opening it up so that the edges of the cut-out rectangles line up together, with the bottom seam in the centre. Pin and sew together.

8 Repeat steps 5–7 for the lining fabric, but this time leave a 3½in (9cm) gap in the centre of the bottom seam.

7

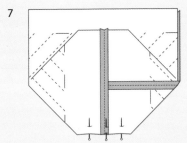

9 Turn the quilted outer part right sides out. Place it inside the lining so they are right sides together, lining up the joining seams. Pin togther to secure.

10 Stitch all the way around the top with a ¼in (6mm) seam.

11 Turn the basket upside down and pull the outer quilted part through the opening in the bottom seam of the lining.

12 Sew the opening in the lining closed, either by hand using a ladder stitch or on the machine, sewing close to the edge and backstitching at beginning and end.

10

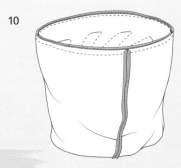

13 Push the lining down inside the outer part. You could add an optional line of hand or machine top stitching around the top, or leave as it is. Turning the top edge over will help the basket keep its shape.

appreciate where you are now

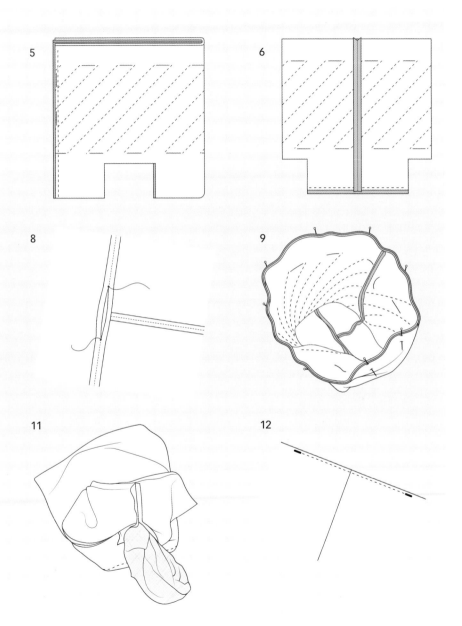

patched pencil case

Small freeform pieced panels are one of my
favourite things to make and this pencil case
(which can double up as a purse or clutch) is a
great way of using them. It is an excellent use
of small scraps of treasured fabrics, as well as
an opportunity to experiment with colour,
shape and texture on a small scale.

Materials
Measures: 8¼ x 4¼in
(21 x 11cm)

- Selection of small
  fabric scraps
- Two 5 x 9in (13 x
  23cm) pieces
  wadding (batting)
- Two 5 x 9in (13 x
  23cm) pieces lining
  fabric
- 8in (20cm) zip (zipper)
- Quilting thread

to make

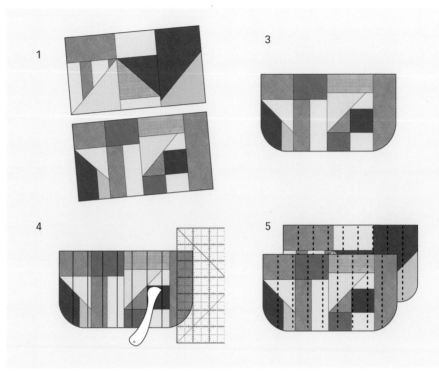

1 Use your choice of freeform piecing techniques and shapes (see pages 30–32) to create two 5 x 9in (13 x 23cm) panels.

2 Baste the patchwork panels to the wadding (batting) using spray baste (see pages 16–17) or a couple of pins.

3 Use a fabric marker to draw around a mug or small bowl to round off the lower two corners of both the basted panels and the lining fabric. Cut away the excess.

4 Mark your quilting lines either vertically or horizontally, 1in (2.5cm) apart, using a Hera marker or similar.

5 Quilt along the lines using your chosen matching or contrasting quilting thread.

6 Prepare the zip (zipper) by folding all four ends of the zipper tape to the back at 45 degrees away from the zip (zipper). Secure in place with a few stitches, either by hand or on the sewing machine.

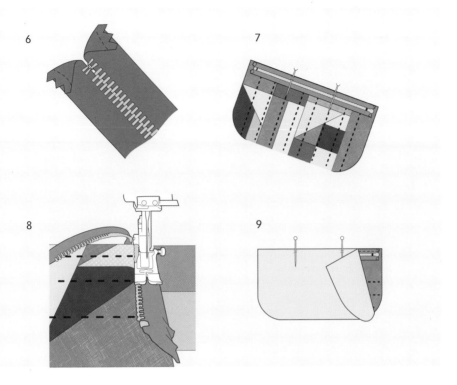

6

7

8

9

7 With one of the quilted panels right side up, centre the zip (zipper) face down along its straight edge and pin in place.

8 Sew the zip (zipper) down, starting from the closed end and aligning the presser foot with the outer edge of the zipper tape. When you reach the zip pull, lift the presser foot and slide the zip (zipper) pull down past the presser foot. Put the presser foot down again and continue sewing to the end.

9 Place a lining panel right side down, covering the zip (zipper) and aligning the raw edge of the lining fabric with the edge of the zipper tape. Pin in place to secure.

10 Sew in place, again keeping the presser foot aligned with the lining raw edge/zipper tape. You are essentially sewing the same seam as before, stopping again to slide the zip pull up before sewing to the end.

11 Flip the attached outer and lining panels wrong sides together so that the unsewn side of the zip (zipper) is exposed. Centre the zip (zipper) right sides together with the second quilted panel. Push the zip pull to the centre and secure either side with pins. Sew along the zipper tape until you reach the zip pull. Stop, lift the presser foot and close the zip. Continue sewing to the end.

12 Add the lining panel as you did before, again starting with the zip (zipper) open, then stopping and closing it once you have sewn a few inches.

13 Open up the pouch so that the outer panels and lining lie wrong sides together either side of the zip (zipper). Use an iron to press the lining fabric away from the zip (zipper) and do the same with the outer panels. Take care not to iron the zip (zipper) itself, especially if you are using a nylon zip (zipper).

14 Beginning at the closed end of the zip, top stitch approximately $1/8$in (3mm) from the seam. Before you get to the zip pull, stop, lift the presser foot and carefully slide the zip pull up behind the presser foot without shifting the pouch too much. Ensure the needle is right above where you stopped sewing, then lower the presser foot and sew to the end. Repeat for the other side.

15 Align the raw edges of the two outer panels and those of the lining right sides together. Pushing the zipper tape towards the outer panels, pin everything in place.

repurpose; renew; relove

10

11

12

13

14

15

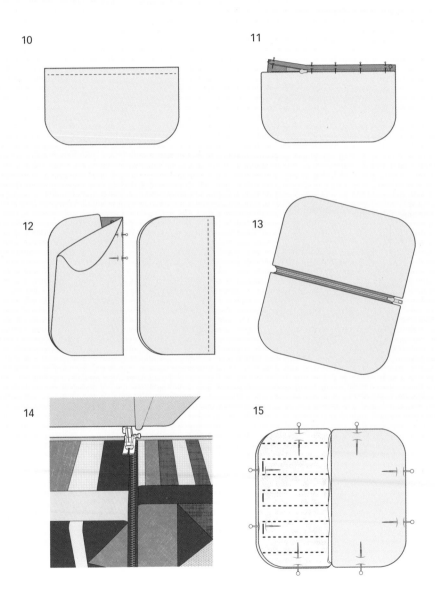

16 On the lining fabric, mark where the ends of the zip (zipper) are and, on the long edge opposite the zip (zipper), mark a 3in (7.5cm) gap in the centre.

17 Beginning at the gap in the lining fabric, sew around the whole outer edge, stopping at the other side of the gap and backstitching at the beginning and end. When you sew the lining, use a $^3/_8$in (1cm) seam allowance. When you reach the zip (zipper), sew back and forth several times over the zipper tape, approximately $^1/_8$in (3mm) from the marked zip (zipper) end. Sew the outer panels with $^1/_4$in (6mm) seam allowance, again sewing back and forth several times when you reach the other end of the zip. Take particular care and sew very slowly over the two zip (zipper) ends where there are multiple layers of fabric.

18 Trim the lining seam allowance to $^1/_4$in (6mm). Trim the seam allowance at each end of the zip (zipper) to no larger than $^1/_8$in (3mm).

19 Reach through the gap in the lining, slide the zip (zipper) open all the way and pull the pouch through the lining gap.

20 Use the blunt point of a pair of scissors to reach through the lining gap and push the closed end of the zip (zipper) out.

21 Tuck the raw edges of the lining gap inside and pin. Sew closed, either by hand using a ladder stitch or on the machine, sewing close to the edge. Backstitch at the beginning and end.

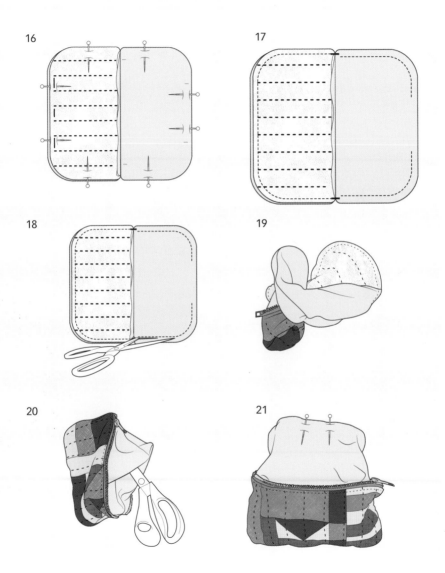

16

17

18

19

20

21

slow stitch pouch

Slow stitching is a playful, creative process that you can make entirely your own. Allow your creativity to flourish, taking time to enjoy the process of slowly adding shape, colour and texture to each panel. The panels are small and portable, perfect for bringing the calmness of slow stitching wherever you are. And the finished pouch is just the right size for carrying your next slow stitch project, tools and materials with you on the go.

Materials

Measures: 8¼ x 9¾in (21 x 25cm)

- Two 11 x 9in (28 x 23cm) outer fabric rectangles
- Two 11 x 9in (28 x 23cm) lining fabric rectangles
- Two 11 x 9in (28 x 23cm) wadding (batting) rectangles
- Selection of small fabric scraps
- 10in (25cm) zip (zipper)
- Quilting thread

to make

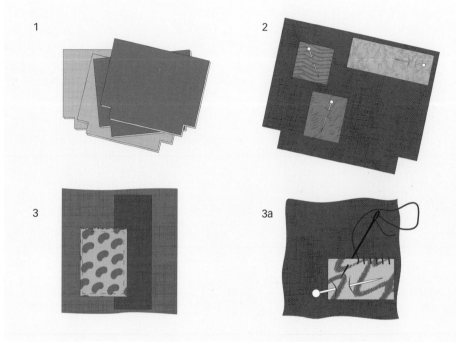

1

2

3

3a

1 Baste the fabric rectangles onto the wadding (batting) using your preferred method (see pages 13–18) and cut a 1¼in (3.2cm) square out of both corners along one long side. Note that any stitching in the strip between the two cut out corners will end up on the base of the pouch.

2 Begin laying your chosen scraps onto your pouch panel. Cut them into any shape you like, either leaving the edges raw or folding them under and pressing, tucking the corners in. There's no need to decide on the position of all the pieces at once – you can just pin and stitch one or two in place, then play around to decide where to add more.

3 There are many ways to stitch your fabrics in place, the easiest of which is a simple running stitch close to the edge of the patch. Here are four more techniques. I encourage you to experiment with other kinds of stitching too.

a Whip stitch around the edge, which can be visible or invisible depending on your choice of thread weight. Bring the needle through from the back, roughly ¹/₈in (3mm) from the edge of the patch. Take the next stitch at an angle, starting horizontally just off the edge of the patch and angling the needle to come up one stitch length above where you started.

3b

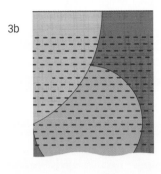

3c

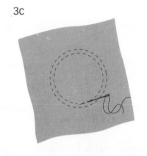

3d

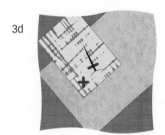

4

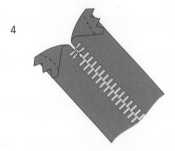

b Quilting stitches, either following a marked design or using freeform stitching. Pin the fabric patches in place and quilt over to secure. You could also use the Baptist Fan template (see page 26) to draw a design or use the plus quilting stitch from the Quilted Coasters (see page 34).

c You can create shapes with your stitches. Here I've marked a circle using the Baptist Fan template (a mug or bowl works well too). Having stitched around the outside line, bring the needle through just inside this line and stitch another circle. Continue until you reach the centre. You could fill the circle with dense straight-line stitches.

d Freeform crosses can add pattern and texture. Bring the needle through to the front, stitch and bring it back through the front about half a stitch to the side of the centre of the first stitch. Take a stitch across the first stitch to form a cross. Repeat in the place where you want to make the next cross.

4 When you have finished both outer panels, prepare the zip (zipper) by folding all four ends of the zipper tape at 45 degrees away from the zip (zipper). Secure in place with a few stitches.

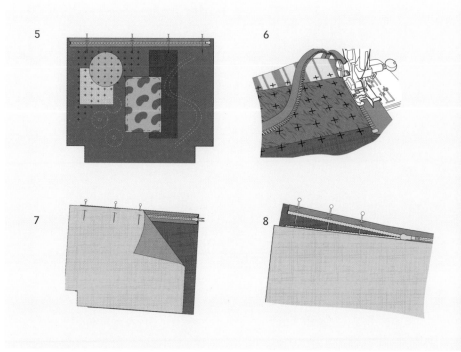

5 Centre the zip (zipper) face down on the quilted panel, aligning the edge of the zipper tape with the raw edge. Pin in place.

6 Sew the zip (zipper) down, starting at the closed end and using a ¼in (6mm) seam allowance. When you reach the zip pull, lift the presser foot and slide the zip pull up past the presser foot. Put the presser foot down again and continue sewing to the end.

7 Place a lining panel right side down, covering the zip (zipper) and aligning the raw edge of the lining with the edge of the zipper tape. Pin to secure and sew in place, again keeping the presser foot aligned with the lining raw edge and the zipper tape. You are essentially sewing the same seam as before, stopping again to slide the zip pull up before sewing to the end.

8 Flip the attached outer and lining panels wrong sides together so that the unsewn side of the zip (zipper) is exposed. Centre the zip (zipper) right sides together with the second quilted panel and secure the corner of the zipper tape with a pin. Because you are now starting at the

9

10

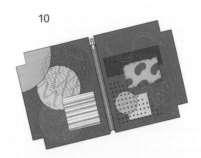

11

12

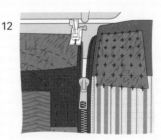

end with the zip pull, begin by pushing it into the centre. Pin and sew around 3in (7.5cm) along the zipper tape, stop, lift the presser foot and close the zip. Continue sewing to the end.

9 Add the lining panel as you did before, again starting with the zip (zipper) open, stopping and closing it once you have sewn a few inches.

10 Open up the pouch so that the outer panels and lining lie wrong sides together either side of the zip. Use an iron to press the lining fabric away from the zip (zipper) and do the same with the outer panels.

11 Beginning at the closed end of the zip, top stitch approximately ⅛in (3mm) from the seam. Before you get to the zip pull, stop, lift the presser foot and carefully slide the zip pull up behind the presser foot without shifting the pouch too much. Ensure the needle is right above where you stopped sewing, lower the presser foot and sew to the end.

12 Repeat for the other side, this time starting with the zip (zipper) open. Stitch a few inches, stop, lift the presser foot, carefully close the zip, lower the presser foot and continue stitching the seam to the end.

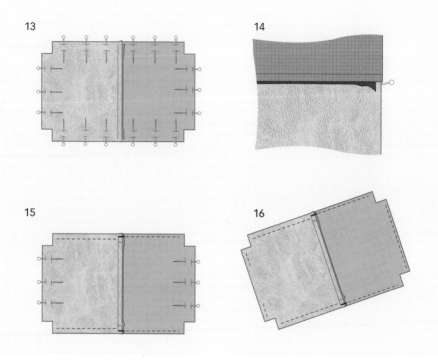

13 Align the raw edges of the two outer panels and those of the lining right sides together. Push the zip pull to the centre of the zip (zipper) and the zipper tape towards the outer panels and pin everything in place.

14 Use an erasable fabric marker to mark a 3in (7.5cm) gap in the base seam of the lining panels. Mark on the lining fabric where the ends of the zip (zipper) are.

15 Sew the side seams, starting from the lining and backstitching at the beginning and end. Use a ³/₈in (1cm) seam allowance for the lining section, then shift to a ¼in (6mm) seam allowance for the outer panels. When you reach the zip (zipper), slow down and sew carefully back and forth a few times, approximately ¹/₈in (3mm) from the closed end of the zip (zipper) and ¼in (6mm) from the open end. You may need to help the fabric through the machine by gently pulling both layers of lining fabric behind the needle.

17

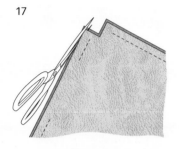

18

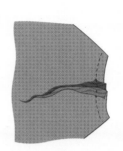

19

20

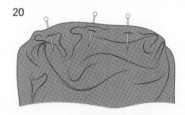

16 Sew the base of the outer panels with a ¼in (6mm) seam. Sew the base of the lining panels with a ³⁄₈in (1cm) seam, leaving the 3in (7.5cm) turning gap open.

17 Trim the lining seam allowance to ¼in (6mm). Trim the seam allowance at each end of the zip (zipper) to no larger than ¹⁄₈in (3mm).

18 Open out the boxed corners of the outer panels and align the two centre seams. Pin in place and sew with a ¼in (6mm) seam allowance. Repeat for the corners of the lining using a ³⁄₈in (1cm) seam allowance.

19 Reach through the gap in the lining, slide the zip (zipper) open all the way and pull the pouch through the lining gap. Use the blunt point of a pair of scissors to reach through the lining gap and push out the closed end of the zip.

20 Tuck the raw edges of the lining gap inside and pin. Sew closed, either by hand using a ladder stitch or on the machine, sewing close to the edge and backstitching at the beginning and end. Tuck the lining back into the pouch and push it into all four corners.

rainbow cross body bag

Materials

Measures: 6¾ x 7¾in
(17 x 20cm)

- Two 9 x 4¾in
  (23 x 12cm) pieces
  of top outer fabric,
  plus one 2.5 x 4in
  (6.5 x 10cm) piece
  for side loops

- Two 9 x 4¾in
  (23 x 12cm) pieces
  of wadding (batting)

- Two 9 x 3½in
  (23 x 9cm) pieces of
  base outer fabric
  (denim, sturdy canvas
  or oilcloth work best)

- Two 9 x 3½in
  (23 x 9cm) pieces of
  interfacing (optional)

- Two 9 x 7½in
  (23 x 19cm) pieces
  of lining fabric

- 5 weight quilting or
  sashiko thread, or
  embroidery floss

- 8in (20cm) zip (zipper)

- 40ft (12m) of ⅛in
  (3mm) cotton cord

- Baptist Fan template
  (see page 26)

A super handy little bag that is just right for carrying all the essentials when you want your hands free. You can either stitch the rainbow with bright, bold colours for those days when you want to make a statement or keep things muted for a more chilled-out vibe. Embroidery thread will really make the colours pop.

to make

1 Baste the top outer fabric panels onto the wadding (batting) using your preferred method (see pages 13–18). Mark the centre at the bottom on each panel and use it as the pin point for the Baptist Fan template (see page 26). Use the template to draw four concentric semicircles, 1in (2.5cm) apart.

2 Quilt the panels, following the drawn design. If the finished panel is slightly distorted from the quilting, trim the long sides straight, without losing too much of the height.

3 If you are using interfacing to reinforce the base panels, fuse it now, then place a base panel and a top panel right sides together and sew. Make sure the top panel is placed so the design is the right way up. Repeat for the second panels.

4 Press the seam allowances up towards the top panels and topstitch from the front with a coordinating thread. Repeat for the second panel. If using oilcloth for the base it will be easier to press the seam allowance down and topstitch on the oilcloth instead.

5 Cut a 1in (2.5cm) square out of the two corners of the base fabric and along one long side of the each of the lining panels.

6 Prepare the side loops by pressing the 4in (10cm) strip of fabric in half lengthwise. Open out and press each of the long raw edges into the centre line. Press in half again and topstitch down each side and once more down the centre. Cut in half to make two 2in (5cm) strips.

7 Prepare the zip (zipper) by folding all four ends of the zipper tape at 45 degrees towards the back and securing in place with a few stitches, either by hand or on the sewing machine.

be bright; be bold

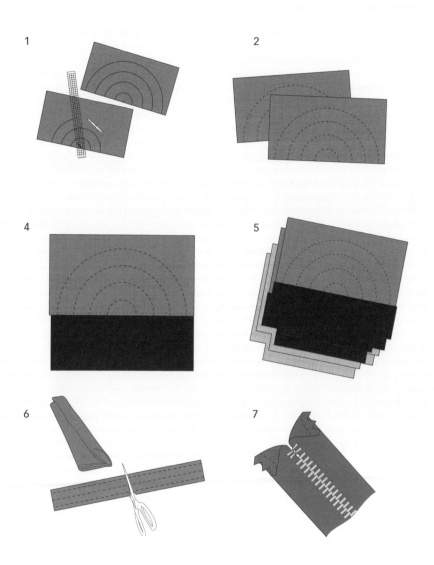

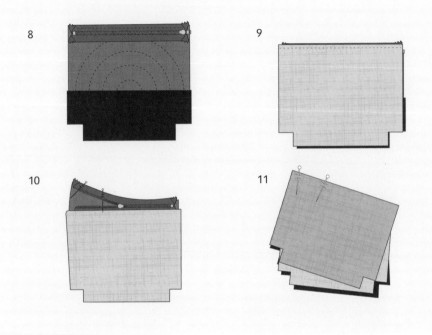

8 Centre the zip (zipper) face down on the quilted panel, aligning the edge of the zipper tape with the raw edge and with the zip (zipper) pull on the right hand side. Pin in place. Starting from the closed end, sew the zip (zipper) down with a ¼in (6mm) seam allowance. When you reach the zip pull, lift the presser foot and slide the zip pull up past the presser foot. Put the presser foot down again and continue sewing to the end.

9 Place a lining panel right side down, covering the zip (zipper) and aligning the raw edge of the lining with the zipper tape edge. Pin and sew in place with a ¼in (6mm) seam. You are sewing the same seam as before, stopping again to slide the zip pull up before sewing to the end.

10 Flip the attached outer and lining panels wrong sides together so that the unsewn side of the zip (zipper) is exposed. Centre the zip right sides together with the second quilted panel and push the zip pull to the centre. Pin in place and sew around 3in (7.5cm) along the zipper tape, stop, lift the presser foot and close the zip. Continue sewing to the end.

11 Add the lining panel as you did in Step 9, but start with the zip (zipper) open and close it once you have sewn a few inches.

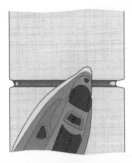

12

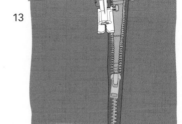

13

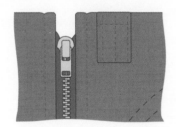

14

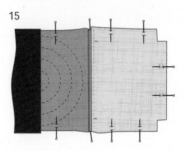

15

12 Open the pouch so that the outer panels and lining lie wrong sides together, either side of the zip (zipper). Press the lining fabric away from the zip (zipper) with an iron. Repeat with the outer panels.

13 Beginning at the closed end of the zip (zipper), top stitch approximately ⅛in (3mm) from the seam. Before you get to the zip (zipper) pull, stop, lift the presser foot and carefully slide the zip pull up behind the presser foot without shifting the pouch too much. Ensure the needle is right above where you stopped sewing, lower the presser foot and sew to the end. Repeat for the other side but start with the zip (zipper) open. Stitch a few inches, stop, lift the presser

foot, carefully close the zip, lower the presser foot and continue stitching the seam to the end.

14 Fold the prepared side loops in half and place ¼in (6mm) down from the top edge, aligning the raw edge with the sides of the outer panel. Sew in place with a short seam and a ⅛in (3mm) seam allowance. Repeat on the other side.

15 Align the raw edges of the two outer panels and those of the lining right sides together. Push the zip pull to the centre of the zip (zipper) and the zipper tape awards the outer panels, pin everything in place. Mark a 3in (7.6cm) gap in the base seam of the lining panels. Mark on the lining fabric where the ends of the zip (zipper) are.

16 Sew the side seams, starting from the lining and back stitching at the beginning and end. Use a roughly 3/8in (1cm) seam allowance for the lining section, then shift to roughly 1/4in (6mm) for the outer panels. When you reach the zip (zipper), slow down and sew carefully back and forth a few times, approximately 1/8in (3mm) from the closed end of the zip (zipper) and 1/4in (6mm) from the open end. You may need to help the fabric through the machine by gently pulling both layers of lining fabric behind the needle.

17 Sew the base of the outer panels with a 1/4in (6mm) seam. Sew the base of the lining panels with a 3/8in (1cm) seam, leaving the 3in (7.5cm) turning gap open. Trim the lining seam to 1/4in (6mm). Trim the seam allowance at each end of the zip (zipper) to 1/8in (3mm).

18 Open out the boxed corners of the outer panels and align the centre seams. Pin and sew with a 1/4in (6mm) seam allowance. Repeat for the lining corners using a 3/8in (1cm) seam allowance.

19 Reach through the gap in the lining, slide the zip (zipper) open all the way and pull the pouch through the lining gap. Use the blunt point of a pair of scissors to reach through the lining gap and push out the closed end of the zip (zipper).

20 Tuck the raw edges of the lining gap inside and pin. Sew closed either by hand using a ladder stitch or on the machine sewing, close to the edge, backstitching at the beginning and end. Tuck the lining back into the pouch and push into all four corners.

21 Make the bag strap by cutting the cord into three 13ft (4m) lengths. Fold each length in half. Make a knot at the looped/folded end using all six cords. Divide into pairs and plait until you have the desired strap length. Before knotting the end, thread the unknotted end up through the first side loop and then down through the second one. Knot the end and trim both ends to a neat tassel to finish.

16

18

19

20

21a

21b

clamshell beach bag

Materials

Measures: 18½ x 20 x 6¾in (47 x 51 x 17cm)

- One 43 x 20in (109 x 51cm) rectangle for bag outer
- 43in x 21in (109 x 53cm) wadding (batting)
- Two 21 x 6in (53 x 15cm) strips for handles
- One 43 x 20in (109 x 51cm) rectangle for bag lining
- One 6 x 7in (15 x 18cm) rectangle for pocket
- Thicker Quilting Thread such as Sashiko or 5 wt pearl cotton
- Baptist Fan template (see page 26)

I love a really big bag for taking all the things to the beach and this bag is exactly that – though it needn't just be for the beach. All but the main construction seams are hand sewn (and those could easily be sewn by hand too), so this project will give you plenty of opportunities for quiet, reflective stitching time. Although the design is traditionally called a clamshell, for me it echoes the rippling waves on a beach, inspiring calming thoughts of the sea.

to make

1 Fold the rectangle of outer fabric in half. Along the bottom, measure 7½in (19cm) in from the fold and mark and cut out a 6in (15cm) wide by 3¼in (9cm) high rectangle, cutting through both layers of fabric. Repeat for the lining fabric.

2 Cut a 1½ x 42in (3.8 x 107cm) strip off the long side of the piece of wadding (batting) and cut in half. Put to one side for the straps.

3 Open up the main piece of outer fabric and stitch or spray baste onto the main piece of wadding (batting). The fabric should overhang the wadding (batting) at the top by ½in (1.3cm). Remove the wadding (batting) from the two cut-out areas.

4 Mark a line 3½in (9cm) from the bottom edge along the whole length of the outer fabric. This is the base line for drawing out your design.

5 Starting from the left, measure 3¼in (8.4cm) in along the base line. Use this as the pin point for the Baptist Fan template to draw three concentric semicircles at 1in (2.5cm), 2in (5cm) and 3in (7.5cm).

6 Measure 3in (7.5cm) along the base line from where the first outer semicircle bisects the base line, pin the template and draw another set of concentric semicircles at 1in (2.5cm), 2in (5cm) and 3in (7.5cm). Continue in this way until you reach the end of the fabric, where the final set of semicircles should fall ¼in (6mm) from the edge of the fabric.

7 Begin the second row of semicircles on the left again. Measure 2¼in (5.8cm) up from the base line in the centre between each set of concentric semicircles and use these points to draw out the next row of concentric semicircles. At either end these will be quarter circles, finishing ¼in (6mm) in from the fabric edge.

let busy thoughts ripple away

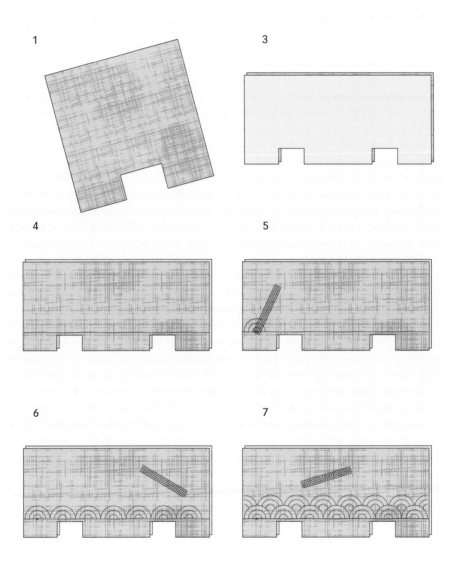

8 For the third row repeat the process as above, this time measuring approximately 4¼in (11cm) up from the base line in-between each set of concentric semicircles and 3¼in (8.4cm) in from the raw edge to create the pin point for the first set of concentric semicircles. The pin point for the remaining semicircles will be approximately 4¼in (11cm) up from the base line in the centre between each set of semicircles in the second row. You might find you need to adjust the pin slightly to ensure the outer semicircles are as close to each other as possible (they will not be touching at this point).

9 Once you have finished drawing out the design, begin quilting it.

10 Once quilted, fold in half, right sides together. Pin and sew the short ends together together with a ¼in (3mm) seam and press open.

11 Rotate the bag so that the seam sits in the centre and the two bottom sections line up. Pin and sew the bottom with a ¼in (3mm) seam and press open.

12 Open up the bottom of the bag so that the corner cut outs lie flat, with the bottom seam in the centre. Pin and sew both seams and press them open. Turn right side out.

13 Press the overhanging ½in (1.3cm) of outer fabric along the top inwards over the wadding (batting).

14 Lay the bag flat with the seam in the centre and use it as a guide to mark the centre of the other side. Then measure and mark 4in (10cm) either side of the centre marks, front and back.

15 Next press the strap fabric pieces in half along the length, wrong sides together. Open up and press both raw edges into the centre fold line.

16 Lift one raw edge and insert a strip of wadding (batting) into each strap, fold the edge over then fold in half along the central fold. Pin in place.

8

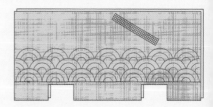

11

14

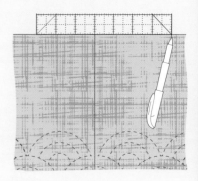

9

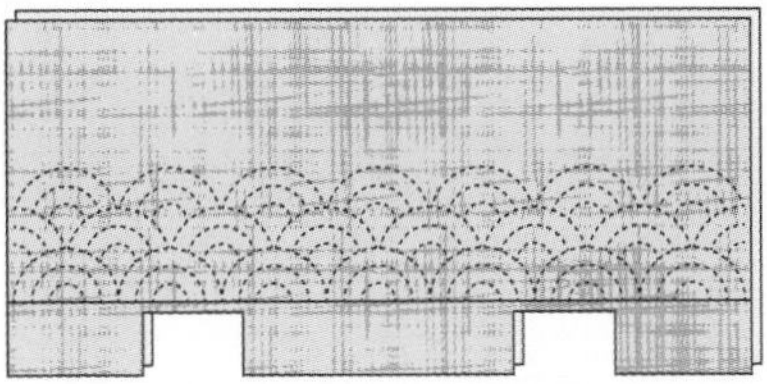

10

12

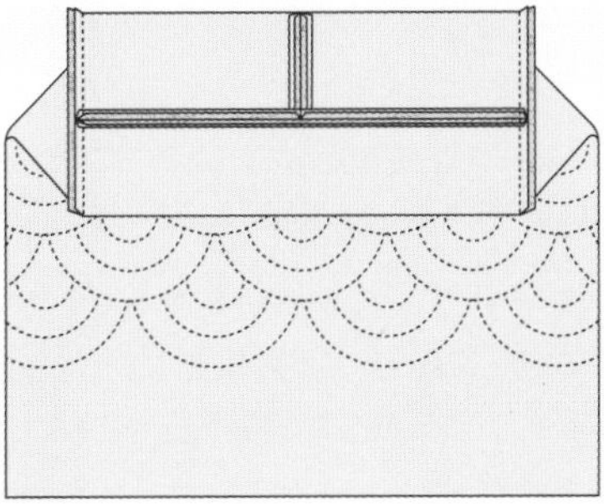

13

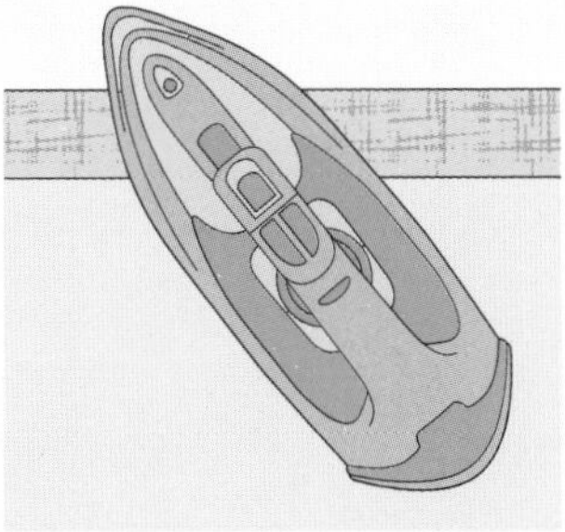

15

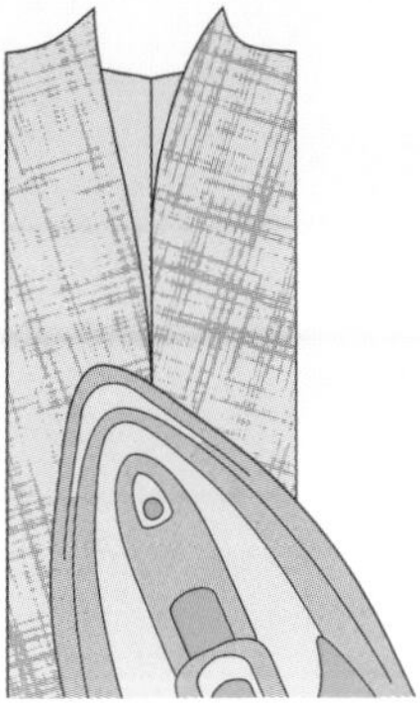

16

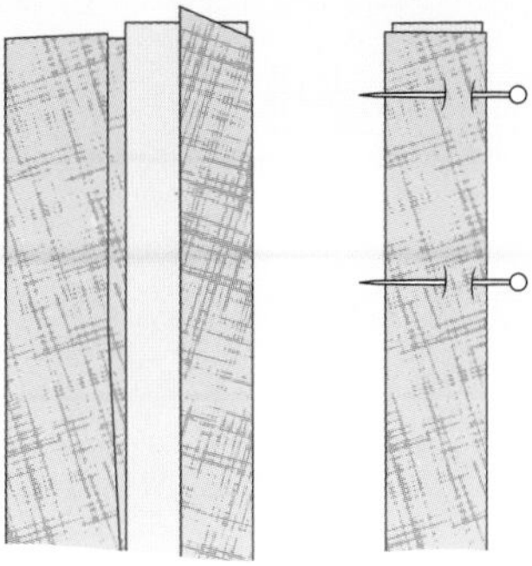

17

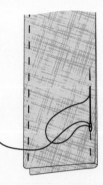

18

20

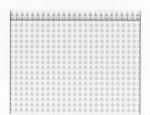

21

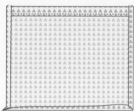

17 Quilt along the pinned side close to the edge, ensuring you go through the wadding (batting) and all four layers of fabric. When you get to the end, take a couple of stitches across the end and continue back along the other side.

18 Mark 1½in (3.8cm) up from each of the short ends of the straps. Ensuring the straps are not twisted, align the 1½in (3.8cm) mark with the top edge of the bag. The inner edge of the strap should line up with the 4in (10cm) mark on the top edge of the bag body. Pin in place.

19 Repeat steps 10–12 to sew the bag lining.

20 Make the pocket from the 6 x 7in (15 x 18cm) rectangle of lining fabric. Fold the top edge over by ¼in (6mm) and press. Fold over again by ½in (1.3cm) and press then stitch in place using a running stitch and quilting thread.

21 Press the remaining three sides in by ¼in (6mm), tuck in the corners and press.

22 Lay the lining flat, right side up, with the centre seam facing upwards. Measure 5in (13cm) down from the top raw edge and pin the pocket in

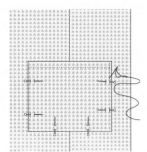

23

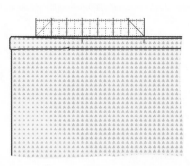

25

place, using the seam to centre it. Stitch in place with running stitch and quilting thread.

23 Press the raw top edge of the lining ¾in (2cm) towards the wrong side. Using the centre seam as a guide, mark the centre of the other side. Mark 4in (10cm) either side of the centre on each side and turn the lining wrong side out.

24 Slide the lining into the main body of the bag and pin them together along the top edge, lining up the centre and 4in (10cm) marks. Ensure the centre seams are both on the same side. The lining should sit just below the edge

of the outer bag. Quilt around the top of the bag, ensuring you stitch through all the layers. You may find you have to take one stitch at a time, especially as you pass through the straps.

25 To secure the straps, mark a 1¼in (3.2cm) square just below the top stitching line that holds each strap end in place. Join the corners diagonally to create a cross. Quilt along these lines: the layers of fabric will make this difficult, so take it slowly. Take a stitch on the front and pull the needle all the way through on the back, before taking a stitch in the back and pulling the needle all the way through to the front again.

coaster cushion

Materials

Measures: 20in
(51cm) square

- Small scraps in two
  colours for the
  'coaster' squares
- Sashing fabric cut to
  the following sizes:
    Twelve 4 x 1½in
    (10 x 3.8cm) strips
    Three 17 x 1½in
    (43 x 3.8cm) strips
    Two 17 x 2in
    (43 x 5cm) strips
    Two 20 x 2in
    (51 x 5cm) strips
    Two 13 x 20½in
    (33 x 52cm)
    rectangles for the
    cushion back
- 21in (53cm) square
  of calico (or any
  unwanted fabric) for
  the inside
- 21in (53cm) square of
  wadding (batting)
- 90 x 2½in (229 x
  6.5cm) binding fabric
- Quilting thread

The inspiration for this cushion came after I laid out some freeform
pieced coaster sets on a linen background – and you could absolutely
use these pieced squares instead of the plain ones in the Qulited
Coasters pattern (see page 34). This is chance to really play with
piecing different shapes: thin strips, triangles, tiny squares or even
curved shapes, if you're feeling bold. Enjoy the mindful process of
moving and rotating the ruler to find the composition of each square
that really speaks to you.

to make

1

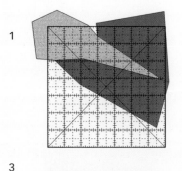

2

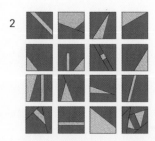

3

4

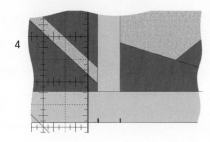

1 Begin by piecing the sixteen 'coasters'.
Be spontaneous – the joy of this process lies in
not planning the layout of each square. Sew two
to four of your scrap pieces together – don't
worry about the size or shape of the final piece,
as long as it is larger than 4in (10cm) square.
Press the seams open. Move the ruler around
until you find a section that you like and cut a
4in (10cm) square. It may be that you can cut
another square from the same piece or perhaps
add another scrap of fabric to the remaining
piece to get another square out of it. Keep going
until you have sixteen 4in (10cm) squares.

2 Arrange the squares in a four-by-four layout.
Take your time finding an arrangement that
really speaks to you. Taking a quick photo is a
good way of seeing how they all work together.

3 When you are happy with your final layout,
begin joining the squares by adding a
4 x 1½in (10 x 3.8cm) strip vertically between
each square to create four rows.

4 Now join the rows by adding a 17 x 1½in (43 x
3.8cm) strip between each row. Once you have
sewn the first strip to the first row, use an
erasable fabric marker to mark the seam lines
of the squares on the other side of the strip.

5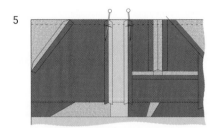

6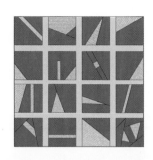

7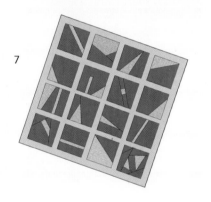

8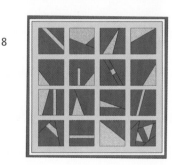

5 Add the next row by aligning the seam lines
   with the marks on the strip. Pin and sew.

6 Continue joining the remaining strips and rows,
   marking the seam lines on the strips and
   aligning the marks with the seam lines.

7 Add the 17 x 2in (43 x 5cm) strips to the top
   and bottom of your rows and then a 20 x 2in
   (51 x 5cm) strip to either side. Press all seams
   open and press again from the front to ensure it
   is nice and flat.

8 Using your preferred method, baste the cushion
   top with the wadding (batting) and calico (see
   pages 13–18).

9   Use a ruler and Hera marker or similar to mark out the quilting lines down the centre of the sashing, which should be approximately ½in (1.3cm) from the edge of the 'coaster' squares. Quilt over the lines.

10 Once you have finished quilting, trim away any excess wadding (batting) and backing fabric, ensuring your panel is 20½in (52cm) square. If it has come up slightly smaller, just ensure it is square and adjust the width of the backing panels accordingly.

11 Now prepare the backing panels. If you choose to piece them from scraps, press the seam allowances to one side and topstitch in place.

12 Fold one of the long raw edges of each backing panel in towards the wrong side by ¼in (6mm) and press. Fold in another ¼in (6mm) and press again. Stitch in place. Repeat for the second panel.

13 Place the backing panels wrong side down onto the back of the quilted cushion square. Align the raw edges with the raw edges of the quilted square, so that the two back panels overlap by about 5in (13cm). Pin and sew in place with a scant ¼in (6mm) seam. Sew back and forth several times over the hemmed edge of the back flap, as this is a point of stress when taking the cushion filler in and out.

14 Follow the double fold binding tutorial in the Useful Techniques section (see page 18) to prepare and attach the binding. Stitch down on the reverse using the ladder stitch method and pop in a cushion insert.

let busy thoughts ripple away

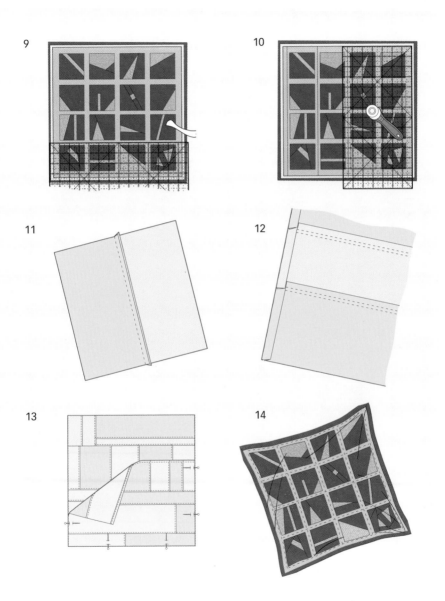

waste not floor cushion

Materials
Measures: 23in (58cm) square

- Scraps and offcuts to create a 23in (58cm) square patchwork top
- Two 13 x 24in (33 x 61cm) fabric panels for the back
- 18–22in (46–56cm) nylon zip (zipper)
- 24in (61cm) square wadding (batting)
- 24in (61cm) square cotton calico (or use fabric you no longer want) for backing

For the insert:
- Two 24in (61cm) squares of cotton calico (or use up fabric you no longer want)
- Small bag of wool or polyester toy stuffing (optional)
- Textile waste, including fabric and wadding (batting) offcuts

No matter how consciously you approach the quilt-making process, it will always generate some textile waste. For me, much of this comes from the collars, cuffs, seams and button plackets of the clothing from which I get my fabric, as well as trimmings from blocks and quilts. Having a separate textile bin on hand makes saving your textile waste easy, and once you have enough it's simple to turn it into cushion inserts. The denser, heavier nature of this material makes it ideal for floor cushions, but it also works fine for regular cushions. You can lighten it up by mixing in a little wool or polyester toy stuffing, or combine it with the insides of your tired, squashed cushions to give them a new lease of life.

move with purpose

to make

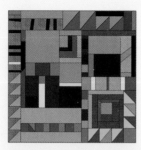

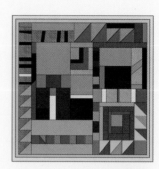

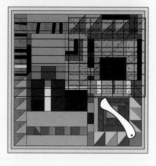

1 Using the freeform patchwork tutorial in the Useful Techniques section (see page 30), make a roughly 23in (58cm) square patchwork panel.

2 Using your preferred basting method (see pages 13–18), baste the panel onto the wadding (batting) and backing fabric.

3 Use a ruler and Hera marker or similar to mark out straight quilting lines across the top, 1¼in (4cm) apart, and quilt.

4 Trim away the excess wadding (batting) and backing fabric.

5 Zigzag stitch (or use pinking shears) along one long side of each of the backing panels.

6 Lay one of the panels flat and centre the zip (zipper) face down along the zigzagged edge. Pin in place and sew with a ¼in (6mm) seam. When you reach the zip pull, stop, lift the presser foot and slide the zip pull away from you, past the presser foot. Put the presser foot down again and sew to the end of the zip tape.

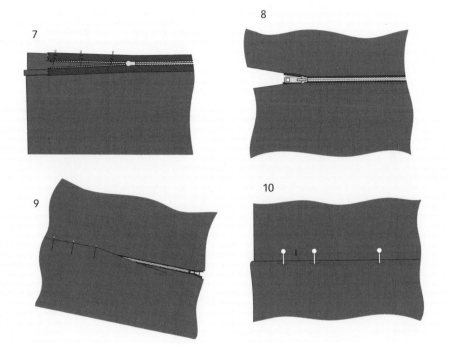

7 Flip the fabric away from the front of the zip (zipper) and place it right sides together with the second panel, aligning the unsewn edge of the zip with the zigzagged edge of the second panel. As you are now starting from the end with the zip pull, open the zip 4–5in (10–13cm), pin just either side of the zip pull and sew as before.

8 Press one of the fabric panels away from the zip (zipper) teeth and topstitch with a coordinating thread.

9 Lay the panels flat face up and use the second panel to create a roughly 1in (2.5cm) folded flap along the length of the panel, covering the zip (zipper) and the line of topstitching. Pin in place.

10 Mark the two ends of the zip (zipper) on the flap and ensure the flap overlaps the lower panel at each end where there is no zip.

11 Sew slowly and carefully along the length of the
flap, approximately 1in (2.5cm) from the fold.
Use your finger to feel for the zip (zipper) teeth
and ensure your seam runs roughly down the
centre of the zipper tape. Stop when you get to
the zip pull, lift the presser foot and slide the zip
open, before continuing with the seam.

12 Sew a short seam along the edge of the flap fold
between the side of the panel and marked end
of the zip (zipper). Backstitch when you reach
the end of the zip. Repeat on the other side.

13 Place the quilted front panel right sides together
with the back panel. Trim the back panel to size
then pin all the way round.

14 Ensuring the zip (zipper) is slightly open, sew a
¼in (6mm) seam around all four sides.

15 Trim the corners, taking care not to cut into the
seam line.

16 Zigzag stitch around all four sides to prevent
fraying. If your machine does not have a zigzag
stitch add a line of straight stitching between
the raw edge and the first seam. Turn right side
out and push out the corners.

making the insert:

1 Sew the two calico squares right sides together
around all four sides using a ¼in (6mm) seam
allowance and leaving a 6in (15cm) turning gap.

2 Sew around all four sides again, this time with
just a little more than a ¼in (6mm) seam
allowance.

3 Turn right sides out and stuff with your textile
waste. How much you stuff it is up to you, but
remember that it will compress over time, so
overstuffed is better than understuffed. Chop
any larger lumpier pieces into smaller ones and
if you are using stuffing, add it a little at a time,
mixing it with the other textile remnants.

4 Once full, tuck the raw edges of the opening in,
pin and hand sew closed.

11

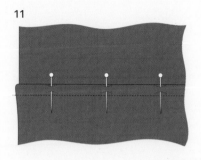

14

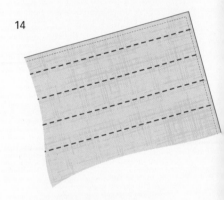

1

12

13

15

16

2

4

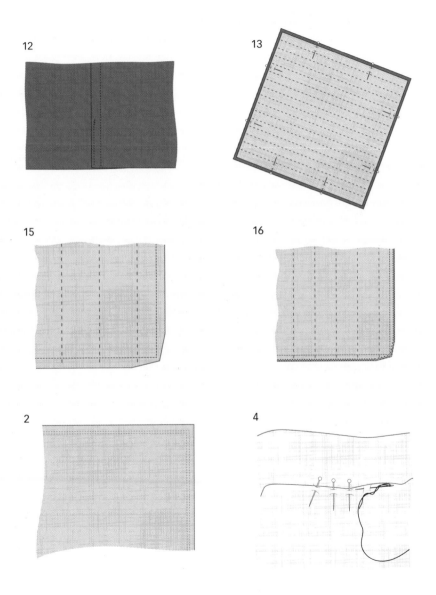

wild fan quilt

This project is perfect for the colder months, when the warmth of the quilt over your lap as you work on it is so appreciated. Once you have basted the layers and drawn out your chosen design, there are just many, many hours of hand stitching to enjoy – truly the epitome of slow stitching. Keep it ready to pick up during quiet moments, even if it's only ten minutes here or there, and let the soothingly repetitive rhythm of the stitches calm even the busiest minds.

Materials

- Front fabric in a size of your choice
- Backing fabric that is minimum 2in (5cm) wider and longer than the front fabric
- Wadding (batting) in the same size as the backing fabric
- Quilting thread
- Baptist Fan template (see page 26)

to make

1 Using your preferred method, baste the fabrics and wadding (batting) together (see pages 13–18), ensuring there is at least 1in (2.5cm) of backing fabric on all sides of the top fabric. If using pins, follow steps 2–4 below before pinning.

2 If the edges of your top fabric are not straight, begin by marking out a rectangle or square the size of your desired quilt, using a Hera marker or erasable fabric marker. There is no need to trim your fabrics or wadding (batting) at this stage.

3 Working inside your drawn square or rectangle, use the Baptist Fan template (see page 26) and an erasable fabric marker to draw out your design. I started in the lower right-hand corner, drawing fans of differing sizes across the whole quilt. You could also opt for a more traditional regular Baptist Fan design or let your creativity go wild – there are no rules here! You could try starting in the centre with a full circle and fan out to the edges, or draw concentric semicircles working from the edges in. If you're unsure, practice your design ideas on paper before drawing them out on the quilt.

4 Once your design is drawn, you can begin quilting. Even if you have not opted for a traditional Fan layout, the Baptist Fan stitching guide (see page 28) may be helpful to maintain continuous stitching. Do not quilt over the lines of the drawn rectangle, stopping and starting your lines of stitching just inside this border.

5 When you have finished quilting, carefully trim away the top fabric and wadding (batting), following the rectangular lines drawn at the start. If the quilting has distorted them slightly, you can straighten them somewhat as you cut, but do not cut through any of the quilting stitches.

6 Trim the backing fabric to leave a border of 1in (2.5cm) around the quilted part.

7 Follow the binding from reverse tutorial in the Useful Techniques section (see page 22) to finish the edges of your quilt. Using the invisible ladder stitch method to sew it down will ensure the quilting design remains intact on the reverse.

8 Wash out the quilt design markings and dry flat. And don't forget to label your work!

reclaim; cherish; restore

border quilt

Freeform patchwork and wholecloth quilting are my two
favourite processes and this large quilt has them in spades.
Making a quilt this size is a labour of love but each part of
the process offers opportunities for bringing creativity and
calm into your day. The patchwork border you'll see in the
illustrations is a chance to really get into the flow of freeform
patchwork piecing, letting the colours and textures of the
fabric speak to you without overthinking their placement.
This quilt is ideal for getting really creative with the back too.
The clean lines of the colourful border on the front can be
let loose in a riotous contrast of scraps brought together for
backing material, as seen here.

Materials
Measures: 75in (190cm) square

- 30½in (77cm) square for
  centre panel
- Fabric scraps for 16 x 10½in
  (41 x 27cm) squares
- Two 12½ x 50in (32 x 127cm)
  border strips
- Two 12½ x 75in (32 x 190cm)
  border strips
- 300 x 2½in (762 x 6.5cm)
  binding fabric
- 74in (188cm) square
  wadding (batting)
- 76in (193cm) square backing fabric
- Baptist fan template one with holes
  1½in (3.8cm) apart (see page 26)

to make

1

2
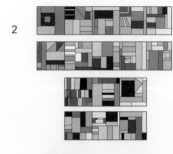

3
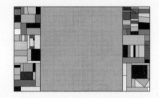

4
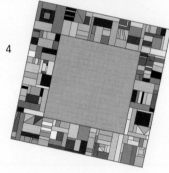

1 Begin by making the patchwork border using the freeform patchwork tutorial in the Useful Techniques section (see page 30). Make up sixteen 10½in (27cm) square blocks.

2 Join the blocks into two sets of three and two of five.

3 Sew the sets of three blocks to either end of the centre square.

4 Join the sets of five blocks to either side of the centre square.

get cosy; be calm

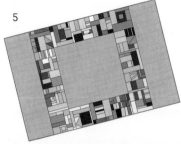

5

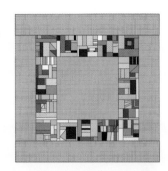

6

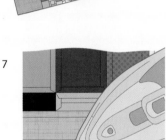

7

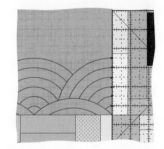

9

5 Next add the outer borders, beginning with the two shorter strips and sewing them to either side.

6 Finally add the longer strips to the top and bottom.

7 Press the quilt top, seams open, from the back and again from the front.

8 Baste the top to the wadding (batting) and backing fabric using the tutorial in the Useful Techniques section (see pages 13–18).

9 First mark out the quilting design in the centre panel. I used the Baptist Fan template (see page 26) to mark out a traditional six arc design, 1in (2.5cm) apart but you could also develop your own more centralized design.

10 Next use a ruler and Hera marker or similar to mark straight lines, 1in (2.5cm) apart, all the way around the patchwork border.

11 Finally mark the quilting design on the outer border. Here I used a Baptist Fan template (see page 26) with holes 1½in (3.8cm) apart. Place the pin point on the corner point of the patchwork border and mark out eight concentric three-quarter circles. If your template is not long enough, use some clear tape to secure an extension to it so that it reaches 12in (30cm).

12 Repeat Step 11 for the remaining three corners.

13 Next, mark a centre point on the seam between the patchwork and outer borders. Use this as the pin point to use the template to mark out a set of eight concentric semicircles using the same 1½in (3.8cm) template. Repeat for the remaining three sides.

14 Quilt the designs. I used a matching pale grey sashiko thread that puts the emphasis on the texture of the quilting. A contrasting thread would shift the focus to the quilting designs, making them more of a feature.

15 Once you have finished quilting, trim away the excess wadding (batting) and backing fabric.

16 Make and attach the binding using the double fold binding tutorial in the Useful Techniques section (see page 18). Sew down on the reverse using a ladder stitch.

17 Wash out the marked quilting designs and dry flat.

10

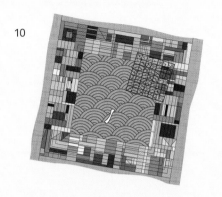

11

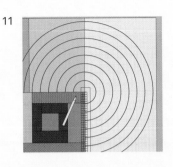

13

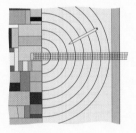

14

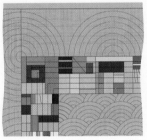

15

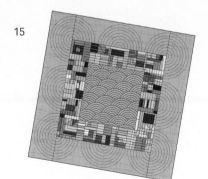

16

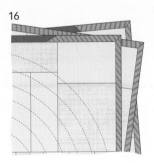

log cabin quilt

The Log Cabin is a traditional quilt design that can be adapted and arranged in any number of ways to create different patterns. Here I've used the 'sunshine and shadows' design, but feel free to play around with the positioning of your blocks to create your own design. For a larger size quilt, simply add more blocks. There is something deeply meditative about the simple repetitive piecing of the blocks. Absorb yourself in the rhythm of sewing, trimming and pressing and feel your mind quieten.

craft for peace; craft for joy

to make

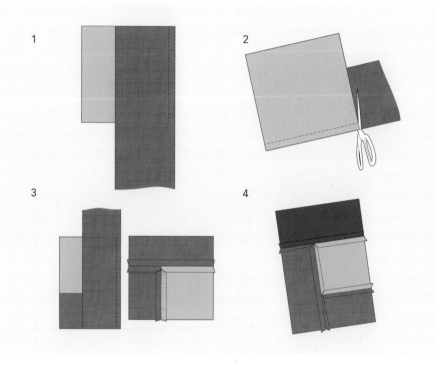

1 Begin with a yellow centre square. Lay a strip of fabric A along one side, right sides together, aligning the raw edges. Sew in place.

2 Flip the fabrics over and, keeping them flat, trim away the remainder of the strip, following the raw edge of the centre square. Finger press the seam open.

3 Working anti-clockwise around the centre square, add another strip of fabric A to the next side. Sew with the new strip on top. Flip over and lay flat to trim away the excess. Finger press the seam open.

4 Continue working anti-clockwise, now adding a strip of fabric B. Flip over, trim away the excess and finger press the seam open.

5 Add another strip of fabric B to the final side of the centre square, sewing, flipping, trimming and finger pressing as before.

6 Continuing to move anti-clockwise around the block, sew a strip of fabric A to the first strip you added in the same way.

7 Sew another strip of fabric A to the next side, a strip of fabric B to the following side and another strip of fabric B to the side after that.

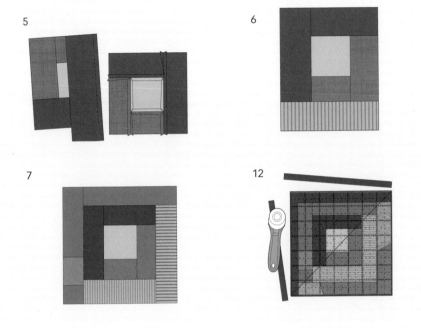

8 In this way, you are building up the block in rounds, each comprised of two strips of fabric A and two strips of fabric B. The finished block must be a minimum of 12½in (32cm) square. If you have used a mix of narrow and wide strips it should take three rounds to reach 12½in (32cm), but if you have only used narrow strips it might take four rounds. Either is fine, as long as you ensure the final strips added are fabric B. You can keep an eye on the overall size of your block as you go around and choose the width of the final round of strips according to what will bring it up to size.

9 If, at any point, your chosen strip is not long enough, simply join one or more pieces of the same width together until it is the right length and add in the same way.

10 Once your block is at least 12½in (32cm) square, press all the seams open with a hot iron from the back and press again from the front.

11 Repeat Steps 1–10 for the remaining fifteen blocks.

12 Trim all the blocks to 12½in (32cm) square. Make sure each of the outer strips are at least ½–¾in (1.2–2cm) wide, otherwise it will be difficult to join correctly.

13 Begin joining the blocks by taking four blocks and arranging them with the fabric A corners in the centre. Join the top and bottom pair and finger press the seams open.

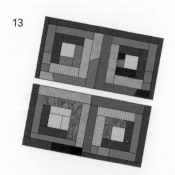

14 Join the two pairs, pinning at the centre seam to keep everything aligned.

15 Repeat for the other blocks to create four extra-large blocks. Join these blocks in the same way as the smaller ones: join into two pairs, then join the pairs to create the quilt top.

16 Baste the quilt top with the wadding (batting) and backing fabric, using your preferred basting method (see pages 13–18). Remember, if you use pins, mark out your quilting lines first.

17 Next mark the quilting lines with a ruler and hera marker or similar. Begin with the centre four blocks by marking a diagonal line from corner to corner of each block to create a square on point, echoing the shapes made by the different colours of fabrics A and B.

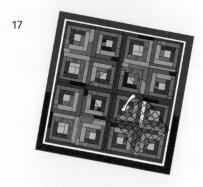

18 Mark another set of lines 3in (7.5cm) in from the first to create a smaller square. Finish with a final set of lines another 3in (7.5cm) in from the second set to create the final square.

19 Repeat the process on all the blue (fabric B) areas around the edge of the quilt. On the sides, this will create three concentric 'V' shapes. On the corners, it will be three diagonal lines.

20 Finally, mark out two concentric squares on each of the four red (fabric A) sections in the same way as you did before. The outer lines are already made, so just mark 3in (7.5cm) in all round for the first square and a further 3in (7.5cm) in for the final square.

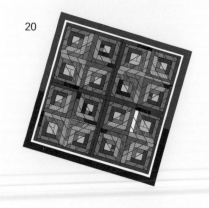

21 Quilt using coordinating threads for each section so as not to detract from the overall design.

22 Trim away the excess wadding (batting) and backing fabric. Bind using the double fold binding technique (see page 18).

14

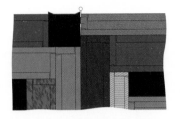

15

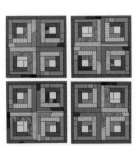

18

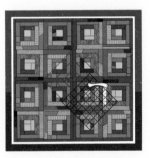

19

21

22

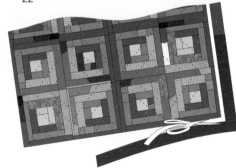

butterfly play quilt

Materials
Measures: 42in (107cm) square

- Twenty-five 9in (23cm) squares for the top
- Various fabric scraps for the butterflies in contrasting colours to the top fabric
- 44in (112cm) square of wadding (batting)
- 46in (117cm) square of backing fabric
- 182in (462cm) binding fabric

This quilt is the perfect size for a baby's play mat but it would work just as well on the wall or as a small lap quilt. Or size it up by adding more squares. Try using different textured fabrics for the 'butterflies' to add a sensory element that small babies would enjoy. Between the simple repetitive piecing of the blocks and the hand quilting this project offers ample opportunities for bringing calmness and mindfulness into your day.

to make

1 From the fabric scraps, cut 32 right-angled triangles with a long side of roughly 4in (10cm). There is no need to be precise in the size of the triangles, but as a rough estimate a 4in (10cm) square divided diagonally into quarters will give you four triangles, and a 3in (7.5cm) square cut diagonally in half will give you two triangles.

2 To make the first block, lay a triangle of fabric right side down across the corner of a front fabric square. Pin and sew in place.

3 Trim away the corner from the front fabric and press the triangle in place with the seam open. Repeat for 22 of the remaining squares, leaving two squares plain.

4 Take nine of the squares with a single corner piece added and repeat Steps 2–3 in the diagonally opposite corner.

5 Trim all 23 squares with added corners back to exactly 9in (23cm).

6 Lay out the squares in a five-by-five grid, as shown in the diagram, with the plain squares in the top left and bottom right corners, single corner squares around the edges and double corner squares in the centre.

reflect and release

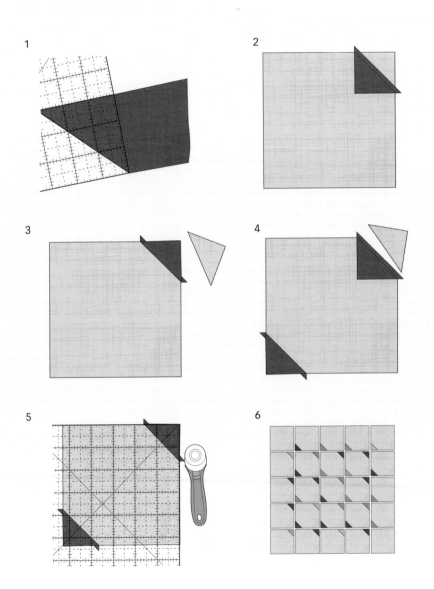

7 Using a consistent ¼in (6mm) seam allowance, begin sewing the quilt top together by joining the squares into five rows.

8 Sew the rows together, lining up and pinning the joining seams between each square. Finger press the seams open at the edge and pin through the stitch line on both pieces to keep the squares aligned.

9 Press the finished quilt top once from the reverse, seams open, and press again from the front to ensure everything is nice and flat.

10 Use your preferred method to baste your quilt top, wadding (batting) and backing fabric together (see pages 13–18).

11 Mark out your quilting lines using a ruler and Hera marker or similar. Start with a diagonal line down the centre by lining up the corner points of the squares. Then work outwards with parallel diagonal lines, approximately 3in (7.5cm) apart, ensuring that every other line runs through the corner points of the squares.

12 Quilt along the marked lines.

13 Trim away the excess wadding (batting) and backing fabric.

14 Follow the double fold binding tutorial in the Useful Techniques section (see page 18) to make and add your binding.

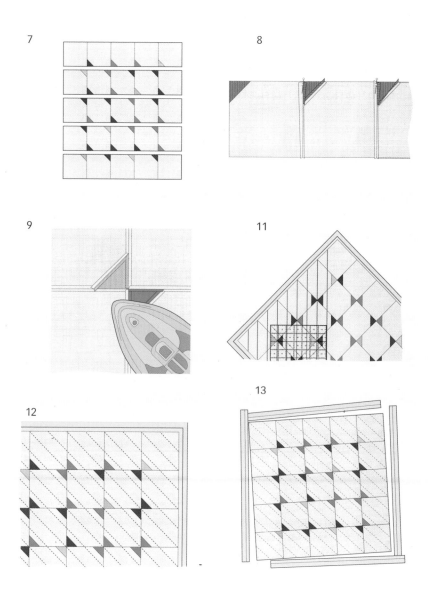

7

8

9

11

12

13

ad astra quilt

Materials

Measures: 52 x 68in
(132 x 173cm)

- 209 squares, 4½in
  (11cm), in shades
  of blue from dark
  to light
- Twelve 4½in (11cm)
  squares in shades
  of yellow
- Twelve 8in (20cm)
  squares in shades
  of yellow
- 255 x 2¼in (6.5m x
  5.8cm) binding fabric
  (or use a selection of
  blue fabrics for
  matching gradient
  binding)
- 54 x 70in (137 x
  178m) wadding
  (batting)
- 56 x 72in (142 x
  183m) backing fabric
  (or piece remnants to
  this size)
- Quilting thread in
  several shades of
  blue and yellow

The wonky star block is a more freeform take on the traditional Sawtooth Star, with its intentional asymmetry making it simpler to construct. While the piecing for this quilt requires more precision than some of the other projects here, it is not complicated. A rotary cutter, cutting mat and quilting ruler will be a worthwhile investment for making this quilt, as the more precisely cut the squares are, the easier they will be to piece with a consistent ¼in (6mm) seam allowance. The focus needed for the construction process works wonderfully to quiet a busy or anxious mind and once the top is finished and basted, then come the many hours of soothing hand quilting.

to make

1 Divide each yellow 8in (20cm) square into eight triangles by cutting it diagonally, horizontally and vertically in half.

2 Beginning with the darkest shades of blue, select eight blue squares in differing shades (some duplicates are fine), one yellow square and eight yellow triangles. This will make up the first block. Lay out the nine squares with the yellow at the centre. If there is some variation in the blue squares, place the darker ones in the bottom row and the lighter ones in the upper row, though a bit of mixing is also fine.

3 The four blue squares directly above, below, to the right and left of the yellow square will have the star points. Begin piecing by laying a yellow triangle across the corner of one of these blue squares and sew down.

4 Fold it up along the seam to check that it entirely covers the blue corner and trim away the blue fabric. Press the yellow corner in place with the seam pressed open. Repeat for the three remaining blue squares.

5 Add the second round of star points by repeating step 3 on the neighbouring corner. Lay across a yellow triangle and stitch down. It does not matter whether the triangle overlaps the first or not.

6 Trim away the blue corner and press up with the seam open. Repeat on the remaining star point squares.

set your intentions

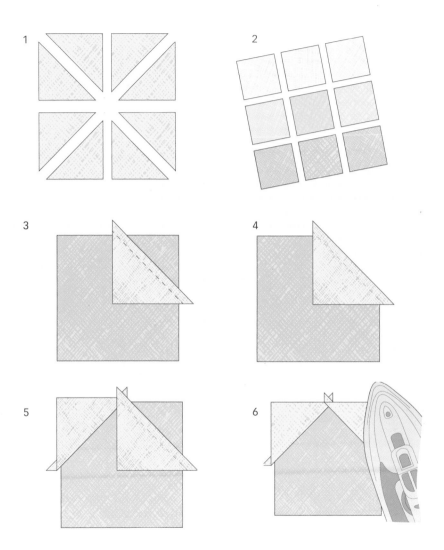

7 Use a ruler to trim the squares back to exactly 4½in (11cm).

8 Reintroduce the squares, now with star points, to your block layout in preparation for sewing together.

9 Lay the top centre square right sides together with the top left square and sew down the right-hand side. Open up and sew the top right square in place in the same way to make a short row.

10 Repeat this process with the centre and lower squares to build three rows.

11 Next join the rows. To ensure the vertical seams line up, finger press the ends of the seams open, carefully line up and pin through both seam lines. Sew together and repeat for the final row. Press the block from the back with seams open and again from the front to ensure it is nice and flat.

12 Repeat the process for the remaining blocks, creating four rows of three blocks in increasingly lighter shades of blue.

13 Lay out all twelve blocks on the floor with an 4½in (11cm) space around each, and begin filling the spaces with the remaining blue squares. Check how the colour gradient is working and choose the remaining blue squares accordingly.

7

8

9

10

11

13

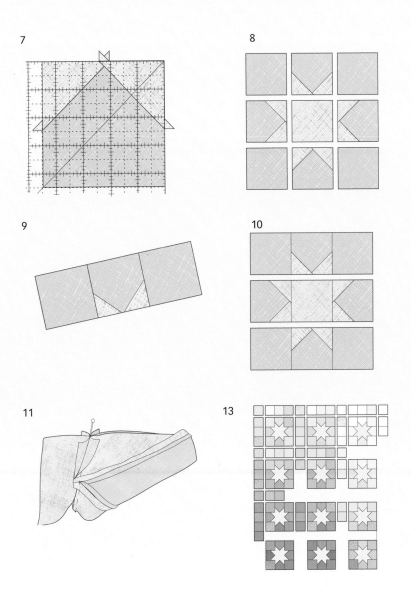

14 Now join the vertical strips of three squares that sit between each of the blocks, as well as those at the beginning and end of each row. Press the seams open.

15 The five longer horizontal strips of thirteen squares can be pieced in the same way.

16 Once you have pieced all the strips you can begin sewing the quilt top together. First add the short strips between the blocks in each row in the same way as you pieced the blocks: matching the seam lines, pinning and sewing in place. Start with a short strip sewn to a block. Open and sew the next short strip to the other side. Open and add a block, followed by a short strip, and so on.

17 You will now have four rows of three blocks, joined with a strip of squares at each end and in-between each block. In the same way as before, now join these rows with the longer strips in-between each row and at the top and bottom. The quilt top will begin to feel somewhat unwieldy as it grows, so take your time, match and pin each seam line and sew carefully. Make sure the weight of the quilt top is either in your lap or on the table next to you so it does not pull your seam lines off as you sew. Press all your seams open with a hot iron on the reverse and again from the front to ensure everything is flat.

18 If you choose to piece the quilt back from remnants do so now, then follow your preferred basting tutorial in the Useful Techniques section (see pages 13–18) to baste your quilt.

19 Quilt the stars in yellow thread, approximately ¼in (6mm) in from the seam line.

20 Add echoing stars in matching or contrasting blue thread in the nine squares that sit in-between the yellow stars. If you wish, draw the quilting lines using an erasable fabric marker, but given the wonky nature of the stars, freehand stitching is fine too. Don't forget the half stars along the sides and quarter stars in the corners.

21 Add a diagonal crosshatch following the unquilted squares. Use a ruler and Hera marker or erasable fabric marker to mark out the lines, and switch thread colours as you stitch each line to keep the gradient.

22 Once you have finished the quilting, lay the quilt out flat and trim any excess wadding (batting) and backing fabric using scissors or a ruler, rotary cutter and mat.

23 Follow the binding tutorial in the Useful Techniques section (see page 18) to attach the binding. If you decide to create your binding in a gradient to blend with the background of the quilt, piece your fabrics as described in the binding tutorial to the correct length.

24 Don't forget to add a label or stitch your name into the quilt.

14–15

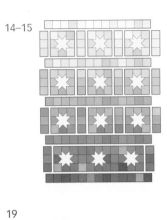

16–17

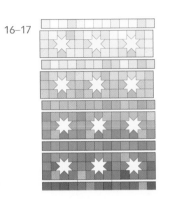

19

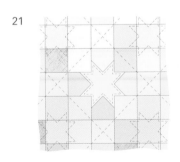

20

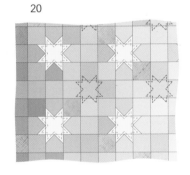

21

22

arrow wall hanging

Materials
Measures: 29¼ x 19¾in
(74.5 x 50.5cm)

- 32 x 21in (81 x 53cm) backing fabric
- 32 x 21in (81 x 53cm) wadding (batting)
- Twenty 17 x 2.5in (43 x 6cm) strips for the top
- 5in (12.5cm) square of top fabric
- 3 x 19in (7.5 x 48cm) strip of fabric for hanging sleeve
- 110 x 2¼in (2.8m x 6cm) binding fabric
- 29½in (75cm) length of string, rope or yarn for hanging
- 20in (51cm) length (minimum) of wooden doweling, bamboo or stick

Quilts are not just for keeping cosy under but make beautiful wall art too. This one is designed specifically for your wall but you can add a hanging sleeve to any size quilt and hang it in the same way. Quilts absorb sound and can really soften a space, bringing a wonderful textural quality to your walls. This wall hanging uses a construction method called quilt-as-you-go that pieces the top whilst also quilting it to the wadding (batting) and backing fabric. The additional hand quilting is not essential but adds that lovely hand quilted texture and the chance to incorporate some slow stitching calm into your day.

to make

3

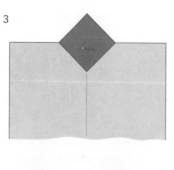

4

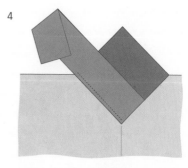

5

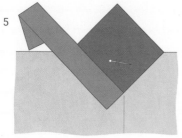

6

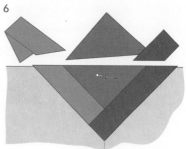

1 Begin by thread or spray basting the backing fabric to the wadding (batting), following the tutorials in the Useful Techniques section (see pages 13–17).

2 Mark a line down the centre along the length on the wadding (batting) side.

3 Take the 5in (12.5cm) square of top fabric and place right side up in the centre, aligning the points with the centre line and the raw edge of the wadding (batting) and backing fabric. Pin in place.

4 Take the first strip of top fabric and lay right side down along one side of the 5in (12.5cm) square. Ensure the end is cut at exactly 90 degrees and lines up with the raw edges of the square below. Pin and sew in place through all the layers. This might feel a little unwieldy at first, with all the wadding (batting) and backing fabric in the way, which is why it's important to pin the strips in place on a flat surface before taking the fabrics to the machine to sew.

5 Press the sewn strip away from the starting square with a hot iron.

7

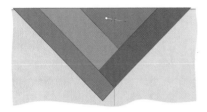

8

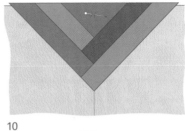

10

9

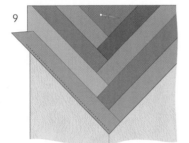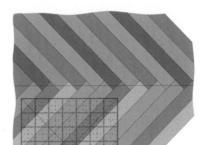

6 Lay the next strip, right side down, along the other side of the starting square, aligning the end with the end of the first strip. Pin, sew and press open as before. Now that both sides of the starting square are sewn down, you can trim away the excess.

7 Take the next strip and lay, right side down, along the raw edge of the first strip, aligning the end with the end of the second strip. Pin, sew and press open. Trim away the excess.

8 Add the next strip to the second side in the same way, aligning the ends, pinning, sewing and pressing open.

9 Continue working your way down the length of the wall hanging, alternating sides and using the marked centre line to ensure you are roughly in line.

10 Once you have added all the strips, mark a new centre line on top of the sewn strips.

11

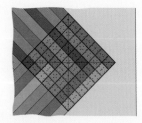

13

14

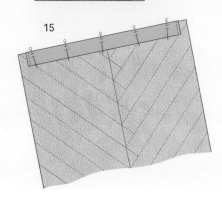

15

11 Use the centre line to square up the wall hanging, trimming away any excess wadding (batting) and backing fabric. Ensure the end point is a 90-degree angle (even if this means trimming the strips slightly), measure 10in (25cm) either side of the centre line and trim the sides and straight end.

12 Mark your quilting lines down the centre of each strip, meeting at the centre line. The strips should be 2in (5cm) wide, so measure and mark 1in (2.5cm) in from the seam line.

13 Quilt along the lines.

14 Next prepare the hanging strip. Fold both short ends in towards the wrong side twice by ¼in (6mm), press and sew.

15 Press in half, wrong sides together, and centre along the top back of the wall hanging, aligning the raw edges. Pin and sew with a ⅛in (3mm) seam allowance.

16 Follow the double fold binding tutorial in the Useful Techniques section (see page 18) to make and add your binding. For the two corners that are larger that 90 degrees, stop ¼in (6mm) from the edge, lift the presser foot and rotate the quilt slightly. Keep the raw edge of the binding aligned with the raw edge of the quilt. This will create a slightly smaller folded triangle, with the fold at an angle, rather than aligned with the upper raw edge as normal. Return to the presser foot, lower and continue stitching the binding down the next side.

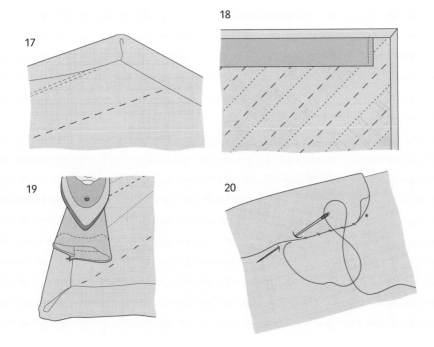

17 When it comes to sewing the binding down on the back, the two wider angled corners will also create smaller mitred corners on the reverse that can be treated as usual with an extra stitch to secure.

18 Stitch the binding as normal over the hanging sleeve.

19 With the top raw edges of the hanging sleeve encased in the binding, open up the sleeve slightly and push up so that the edge sits just below the outer edge of the binding. Press with a hot iron.

20 With a fine coordinating sewing thread, hand stitch the lower fold of the hanging sleeve to the back of the quilt. Bury the knot under the hanging sleeve, then with each stitch, catch a small amount of the hanging sleeve and a larger length of backing fabric. Take care not to stitch through to the front. Bury the knot under the sleeve when you reach the other end.

21 Slide the wooden doweling, bamboo or stick through the sleeve and knot the string at each end at your desired length. Hang and enjoy!

handwork is heartwork

sunny days
patchwork curtain

When I designed this curtain, I imagined it blowing in the breeze from an
open window with the sun streaming through it creating a magical
stained glass effect from the patchwork seams. It's a tab top style, so
requires only a single curtain pole to hang from. You can keep it simple
with neutral fabrics or add a splash of colour with something bolder and
brighter. This is not technically a quilting project but you could easily add
some stitching to it, particularly if you use large, plain fabric pieces and
want to add some interest. I have not given measurements for the
curtain, as the finished size depends on to the space you have to fill.

Materials

- Selection of larger
  fabric scraps and
  remnants
- Piece of lightweight
  cotton gauze the size
  of your curtain
- 6 x 8in (15 x 20cm)
  fabric rectangles for
  the tabs at the top
  – you will need
  approximately one
  for every 6in (15cm)
  of curtain width
- Quilting thread
  (optional)

to make

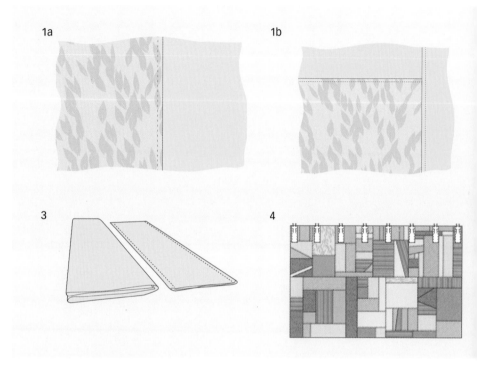

1a

1b

3

4

1 Piece the curtain top, following the freeform patchwork tutorial in the Useful Techniques section (see page 30), but with one key difference: after sewing each seam, press both seam allowances to one side with an iron and topstitch them down before adding the next piece. Work to create large slabs of patchwork, straightening the edges with a ruler before joining them to create the finished curtain top.

2 When the top has reached your chosen size, trim the edges to a neat square or rectangle.

3 Prepare the hanging tabs by folding each in half and pressing. Open it up, fold the two raw edges in to the centre and fold in half again. Press and top stitch down each side.

4 Fold the tabs in half and pin to the right side of the curtain top, aligning the raw edges of the tabs with the raw edges of the curtain. The tabs should be ¼in (6mm) in from each end, then distributed every 6in (15cm) along the top edge.

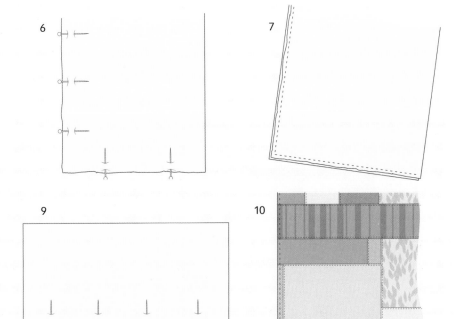

5 Sew a line of basting stitches along the top edge of the curtain to secure the tabs using a ⅛in (3mm) seam allowance and the longest stitch length on your machine.

6 Lay the lightweight cotton gauze right sides together over the patchwork top. Mark a 8in (20cm) turning gap in the bottom edge (if possible, avoid placing the gap over a seamed section) and pin all the way around.

7 Sew all the way around the edge with a ¼in (6mm) seam, leaving the turning gap open. Take care not to catch the sides of the tab loops as you sew the side seams of the curtain.

8 Pull the curtain right side out through the turning gap.

9 Tuck in the raw edges of the turning gap, press and pin. Press all the way around the edge of the curtain to create a neat straight edge, ensuring that none of the backing fabric is visible from the front.

10 Topstitch all the way around the edge of the curtain, closing the turning gap in the process. If you wish to add any quilting, do so now, otherwise hang in a sunny window and enjoy.

plus cushion

The beautifully simple plus stitch is one I use
often in my own work and here it adds
interest and texture to this simple cushion.
You could opt to keep things clean with plain
linen and contrasting thread or give it a
different look with a printed fabric or some
simple pieced scraps. Whatever you choose,
take time to enjoy the gentle repetition of the
stitching process that is perfect for bringing a
little calm into your day.

Materials
Measures: 18½in (47cm)
square

- 20in (51cm) square
  for the front
- Two 13 x 19in
  (33 x 48cm)
  rectangles for
  the back
- 20in (51cm) square
  wadding (batting)
- 20in (51cm) square
  lightweight
  interfacing (optional)
- Contrasting quilting
  thread
- 20in (50cm) cushion
  insert